IAN FLEMING'S SECRET WAR

by

Craig Cabell

Pen & Sword
MILITARY

First published in Great Britain in 2008
and reprinted in this format in 2016 by
PEN & SWORD MILITARY
An imprint of
Pen & Sword Books Ltd
47 Church Street
Barnsley
South Yorkshire, S70 2AS

ISBN 978 1 47385 349 2

Printed and bound in England by
CPI Group (UK) Ltd, Croydon, CR0 4YY

Typeset in Palatino by
Phoenix Typesetting, Auldgirth, Dumfriesshire

Pen & Sword Books Ltd incorporates the imprints of Aviation, Atlas,
Family History, Fiction, Maritime, Military, Discovery, Politics, History,
Archaeology, Select, Wharncliffe Local History, Wharncliffe True Crime,
Military Classics, Wharncliffe Transport, Leo Cooper, The Praetorian
Press, Remember When, Seaforth Publishing and Frontline Publishing.

For a complete list of Pen & Sword titles please contact
PEN & SWORD BOOKS LIMITED
47 Church Street, Barnsley, South Yorkshire, S70 2AS, England
E-mail: enquiries@pen-and-sword.co.uk
Website: www.pen-and-sword.co.uk

Contents

For Samantha, Nathan and Fern –
make your dreams come true.
And to Anita, Berny and Dave –
for all the support over the years.

Preface

'. . . God laughed through her mouth . . . a lovely yet terrible sound.'
I, Claudius – Robert Graves

For fifteen years I have spoken to antiquarian book dealers concerning collectible British authors. Some never go out of fashion, such as Charles Dickens, Agatha Christie, J.R.R. Tolkien and Ian Fleming.

When one reads the blurb in these authors' books, one marvels at the lack of imagination employed by the publisher when describing their star-writer. The same things crop up time and again, which does nothing but make the initiated squirm and the uninitiated shrug their shoulders. That said, I always found the odd line concerning Ian Fleming's life in the Naval Intelligence Department (NID) of interest because I had spent a pleasant year at Old Admiralty Building, Whitehall, myself. One day, while looking through the archives there, I found an old promotions record dating from the Great War and marvelled at the amount of information the military kept locked away. Surely there was more to say about Fleming's time in NID than could be said in the bland blurb of a book?

Clearly there was. Several biographies of Fleming documented broadly his war years. This made interesting reading, but surely more could be said than that?

After picking up the Royal Society of Literature's copy of

Dennis Wheatley's war papers for the Joint Planning Staff of the War Cabinet (*Stranger Than Fiction*, Hutchinson 1959), I became fascinated in writers' abilities to work in a staunch military environment during times of crisis. My book *Dennis Wheatley – Churchill's Storyteller* became a fascinating book to research and write. The name Peter Fleming (Ian's brother) cropped up from time to time, but I only referred to him once. But when I found literature concerning Ian Fleming and his activities during the war, fresh from writing the Wheatley book, I instantly noticed a few things that had been reported incorrectly before; mainly on the internet. This got me interested in writing a sister-work to my Wheatley book. A piece of non-fiction concerning Ian Fleming's covert activities during the Second World War. I approached Pen & Sword and they instantly agreed; both of us blissfully unaware that my publication would coincide with the Ian Fleming Centenary.

That said, *Ian Fleming's Secret War* was not an easy book to write. Although there is a wealth of information in the National Archive, some signed in Fleming's fair hand, there are gaps in the information, which is, to say the least, frustrating.

I have endeavoured to fill in those gaps, looking at specific operations and events as individual case studies in this book. I do believe wholeheartedly that I have taken the understanding of Ian Fleming's war years a couple of steps forwards by dealing with each subject in isolation rather than bouncing backwards and forwards.

That said, there are still some frustrating holes, specifically, in regard to Fleming's two trips to America. For me, there seems to be a lack of first-hand documentation. Maybe not even that, maybe there's something that doesn't sit quite right with me concerning the nuances of the trip – probably more on Admiral Godfrey's side than Fleming's – maybe some of the answers can be found in America; but what I had to remind myself of while writing this book is:

it's about Ian Fleming and what he achieved during the war, not everyone else. As soon as everyone else becomes involved, Fleming becomes lost.

That said, an area I had to explore with the bare minimum of Fleming input was Rudolf Hess' flight to the UK. There are many people who accuse Fleming of having a hand in this strange incident and for one reason alone – Fleming's contact with Aleister Crowley – I have some sympathy with that. Like many intelligence operations during the Second World War, I feel that the Hess case has fingers from many pies in it. I pull the story together from my own point of view, discussing Ian and Peter Fleming in relation to Dennis Wheatley and Aleister Crowley, in what I believe to be a credible hypothesis. I make no apology over the subjectivity of this chapter as I feel it highlights the frustrations of writing about British intelligence work of the mid-twentieth century. I can only assure the reader that I have pulled the facts together the best way I could with regard to this chapter, but there is still some supposition. That said, I haven't twisted the facts to suit the theories.

I have refrained from supposing away in other areas of the book. For example, I believe an in-depth study of the workings of 30 Assault Unit in regard to Operations CROSSBOW, BIG BEN and PAPERCLIP (the whole of the V rocket operations) is needed. Although I have kept my facts to Operation CROSSBOW and to a small degree BIG BEN, I did not venture into PAPERCLIP, which is a vast area and one for which I couldn't find any significant documentation (in the National Archive appertaining to 30 AU activity) or, more importantly, any relevance to Ian Fleming, so left it alone. However, the revelations of the veterans did inspire me to look more closely at the work of Fleming and 30 AU in comparison to interesting links in the Bond novel *Moonraker*.

There is a wealth of information concerning Operation GOLDENEYE in the National Archive. The nuances of the construction of the operation in Europe by Fleming needs meticulous handling and demands a substantial book in its own right. Perhaps it will make more of a challenging read; but the diplomatic relationships, background intelligence and results of putting the operation at readiness, is something that would deeply interest the military scholar. In this book I address Operation GOLDENEYE as a stand alone chapter, outlining its aims: broadly Fleming's work and 'lessons learned' afterwards. I am content that it has addressed most of the workings of the operation but do not wish to over-egg my findings. There is more information in the archive and publication should be arranged for a specific audience in mind.

The details of Ian Fleming's war are far reaching and I have made the decision to keep things as tight as possible. By dealing solely with Fleming's work – and that of 30 AU – there will be a criticism that I have ignored his home life and other social activities. This was all quite deliberate because I believe interest in this area of Fleming's life come together more affectively in a book that looks at the larger canvas of his life. In short, a full biography. What you have here is a snap shot of a job Ian Fleming did for the five years of the war, working for Naval intelligence. That said, I did find myself referring to incidents and novels appertaining to James Bond, because there was so much relevance there, let alone some of the real-life people from Fleming's war years who would influence those characters.

It is right that we celebrate Ian Fleming's life for his wonderful books, from *Casino Royale* to *Chitty, Chitty, Bang, Bang* (and let us not forget his non-fiction such as *The Diamond Smugglers* and *Thrilling Cities*); but let us not lose sight of the wonderful contribution he made to the war effort too, pushing the boundaries of a largely administrative job into something much more magical – something that gave him so much fulfilment and paved the way for the spy stories to end all spy stories: those fourteen James Bond novels and short-story anthologies that have been turned into over twenty movies.

Everybody has many facets to their personality, so here is a glimpse of gold from Ian Fleming's.

Craig Cabell
London
February 2008

Acknowledgements

I would like to thank the staff of the National Archive, Kew, for their patience, professionalism and for dealing with all my teething problems with the new system. I would also like to thank the staff of the following establishments who helped me when I followed-up tiny snippets of information associated with Fleming's wartime antics: the Imperial War Museum with regard to photographs, Bletchley Park, the National Maritime Museum, the Cabinet War Rooms, Whitehall Library, Eltham Library, the National Portrait Gallery, and Old Admiralty Building (down to the dungeon).

Thanks are also due to Kate Grimond who read the manuscript on behalf of the Fleming Estate. A big thank you to the veterans of 30 AU who gave their time to talk to me, especially James 'Bill' Powell and Bill Thomas. Many thanks to E.J 'Ted' Poole for his superb artwork and generosity, Allan Farrin for his time, comments and excellent website showcasing 30 Assault Unit www.30au.co.uk (I'm sorry I didn't use it); and to Keith and Penny at The Marine, Littlehampton (the spiritual home of 30 AU), thanks for your kindness and support; your dedication to the lasting memory of the unit is exemplary.

I would also like to thank: Admiral Malcolm Rutherford, Captain Melly, Captain Paul Robinson, Commander Lunn and Captain 'Spike' (*Heartbreak Ridge*) of HMS *Grafton*, David Waters, Steve Kerchey, for allowing me my own glimpse of the Royal Navy over the past fifteen years – great men, all, who I never had a cross word with not even once. And thank you to my dear friend Steve Moore for the quality information from a quirky source, you're really one of the best dear friend. And John Collins, another great friend, who provided quality information.

Thank you to actor Christopher Lee for his memories, His Grace the 15th Duke of Hamilton in regard to Rudolf Hess' last flight, also Lyndsay J Stuart. A special thank you to Simon Wiesenthal for the opportunity to converse, Lord Greville Janner for his conversations concerning Nazi War Criminals, Frederick Forsyth for his professionalism, advice and support of my many projects, General Sir Mike Jackson for some autobiographical inspiration, the Estate of Dennis Wheatley for their assistance, Richard Overy for his most excellent work *Interrogations, the Nazi Elite in Allied Hands, 1945*, Thaddeus Holt for *his* most-excellent *The Deceivers, Allied Military Deception in the Second World War*, Georgina Godden for a lesson in French grammar, Charles Hewitt, Henry Wilson and Jonathan Wright at Pen & Sword Books Limited for making the journey less troublesome (one of the better small publishers), Crispin Jackson and Jonathan Scott, the previous editors of *Book and Magazine Collector* for their time and trouble, Nigel Williams Rare Books and Richard Platt of The Bookshop on the Heath for consultation on the Collector's Guide and always being polite, frank and honest, my father Colin for the Noel Coward sound bites, Group Captain Jim Spurrell for all things associated with protocol and the odd cool word when wisdom above my years was needed (a real unsung hero that man), my great friend Tony Mulliken for the odd breakfast meeting and more food-for-thought than I could dare follow up, Mark Ottowell, Graham A. Thomas and David Barlow for believing in the project from the word go, your support, and the Waipara, really helped, as ever! And Steven White for getting back in touch; you were always great to bounce historical ideas off, dear friend.

Thanks also to my wife Anita, for putting up with yet *another* book and hearing all about it, your patience is a virtue, and thanks are due to a 'good friend' for quality discussions concerning Small Arms and Commander Bond – in the UK and the Middle East (wherever you are!).

Thanks go to Neil and Frances for their kind support when the computer failed, I truly appreciate it and Wayne Shorter for fixing the 'damn thing' when others couldn't.

Eternal thanks also to my children for wanting milk and biscuits when I was 'fighting them on the beaches', we all need a little distraction – don't we!

Craig Cabell
London, February 2008

Dramatis Personae

(a list of some key players outlined in this book)

Lieutenant-Colonel John Bevan – Stockbroker and Dennis Wheatley's boss in the Joint Planning Staff (JPS)

Staff-Sergeant Bramah – Crashed glider pilot who worked with French Resistance and 30 AU

Major W. G. Cass – Original second-in-command of 30 AU

Jock Colville – Friend of Fleming who worked as a secretary in the FO

Surgeon-Lieutenant Dr Bruce Cooper – Volunteer from Shortly (naval school) for Operation TRACER

Aleister Crowley – Occultist who offered his skills to British intelligence during the Second World War

Commander Dunstan Curtis – Dalzel-Job's boss 30 AU

Patrick Dalzel-Job – Intelligence Officer and member of 30 AU (and possibly the inspiration for the character of James Bond)

Sefton Delmer – Journalist and member of the Naval Intelligence Department (NID)

William Joseph Donovan – Officer from the American Office of Strategic Services (OSS)

Captain Charles Drake – Retired Officer and member of NID

Ian Lancaster Fleming – Writer, stockbroker and commander Royal Navy Voluntary Reserves (RNVR)

Peter Fleming – Ian's brother, and officer in British Intelligence, London Controlling Section (LCS) etc.

Brigadier Gambier-Parry – M16 radio expert (Operation TRACER)

Rear Admiral John Godfrey – Director of Naval Intelligence (DNI) 1939–42

Olaf Hambro – Chairman of Hambros Bank

Robert Harling – No2 to Lieutenant Donald McLauchlan in NID

Rudolf Hess – Deputy Fuhrer of the Third Reich who made a flight from Augsburg to Scotland on 10 May 1941

Captain Alan Hillgarth – Former consul of Majorca who became military attaché of Spain prior to Operation GOLDENEYE

Admiral Aubrey Hugh-Smith – Naval Intelligence (and brother of Lancelot Hugh-Smith senior partner in Fleming's employers Rowe & Pitman)

Albrecht Georg Haushofer – Long term friend of Rudolf Hess and contact of British intelligence

Ralph Izzard – 30 AU V rocket expert

Surgeon-Commander Murray Levick – Formerly part of Captain Scott's last expedition to the Antarctic, he would be Admiral Godfrey's main trainer for staff in Operation TRACER

Lieutenant Donald McLauchlan – Former journalist and propaganda desk officer NID

Commander Ewan Montagu – Author of *The Man Who Never Was* and NID desk officer, who left the department to join the Twenty Committee

Montagu Norman – Governor of the Bank of England

Edward Peacock – Head of Barings Bank

Commodore E G N Rushbrooke – Took over from Godfrey as DNI

Commander 'Red' Ryder – Original commander of 30 AU

Otto Skorzeny – Nazi expert in special operations techniques. Influenced Fleming in the creation of 30 AU

Sir William Stephenson – Contact of Fleming's who was head of British Security Coordination (BSC), USA

Dennis Wheatley – Squadron Leader and later Wing Commander, JPS/London Controlling Section and acquaintance of the Fleming brothers

Sir William Wiseman – Predecessor to William Stephenson, as head of BSC, USA

Lois de Wohl – Austro-Hungarian Astrologer whose skills were employed by areas of NID

Bill Wright – Bodyguard of Dalzel-Job in 30 AU

List of Abbreviations

30 CU	30 Commando Unit (rather than 30 Commando or Special Engineering Unit, became 30 AU)
30 AU	30 Assault Unit
BSC	British Security Coordination
COI	Co-ordinator of Information
CoS	Chiefs of Staff
DNI	Director of Naval Intelligence
FBI	Federal Bureau of Investigation
FO	Foreign Office (later the Foreign and Commonwealth Office – FCO)
JIC	Joint Intelligence Committee
JPS	Joint Planning Staff
LCS	London Controlling Section
MI R	Military Intelligence Research
MoD	Ministry of Defence
NID	Naval Intelligence Department
OSS	Office of Strategic Services
PWE	Political Warfare Executive
RM	Royal Marines
RN	Royal Navy
RNVR	Royal Navy Voluntary Reserves
SIS	Secret Intelligence Service
SOE	Secret Operations Executive
VCIGS	Vice Chief of the Imperial General Staff

Note on the Text

There is a tendency with works connected to the Second World War to tar the German people with the crimes of the Nazi party. I find this intolerable and therefore deliberately distinguish, in my work, between 'German people' and 'Nazis' (the only exception being some quotes that refer to 'Germans', which I have left unaltered).

I have had the honour and privilege to work, converse and talk to distinguished people connected with the plight of the Jews during the Second World War, including Simon Wiesenthal, Lord Greville Janner of Braunstone and other members of the World Jewish Congress. Although this book does not focus strongly on this subject or, make sweeping statements about the Nazis and their war crimes, it is still there (especially in certain individual's attitudes and make-up). I would like to state, from the outset, my treatment of the Nazis, from an historical context, is damning and I place them as a separate entity from the German people who, as a whole, and, individually, I respect greatly.

I feel there is a need in 2008, as the Second World War becomes more historical fact than common memory and the hunt for Nazi war criminals comes to a close, to remind ourselves who the bad guys really were. So many German people were victims of war crimes, from rape and torture to execution; it is extremely hard to make a contemporary audience aware of such things unless highlighted early on in any work connected to the Second World War.

Things are never black and white, there are many shades of grey, so do not tarnish the German people with the crimes of some of their forefathers, but understand the complex web that Adolf Hitler and his henchmen created in order to terrorise Europe. German Jews, German homosexuals and German disabled met the same fate as their kin wherever the Nazis went and please do not forget that.

One last thing: the Diary of Solomon Tauber, from Frederick Forsyth's masterpiece *The Odessa File*, is a real diary loaned to the author by Simon Wiesenthal; so the truth is much stranger than fiction as, you will learn throughout this book.

'I bear no hatred nor bitterness towards the German people, for they are a good people. Peoples are not evil; only individuals are evil.'

The Diary of Solomon Tauber
The Odessa File
Frederick Forsyth

Craig Cabell,
London,
February 2008

Introduction

'The second course came, and with it a bottle of Kavaklidere, a rich coarse burgundy like any other Balkan wine. The kebab was good and tasted of smoked bacon fat and onions. Kerim ate a kind of Steak Tartare – a large flat hamburger of finely minced raw meat laced with peppers and chives and bound together with yolk of egg. He made Bond try a forkful. It was delicious. Bond said so.'

From Russia with Love

Novelists have a natural capacity for lateral thought because of their creative natures. When that skill is employed in a real-life military environment, an extra dimension is gained: creative strategy. A good example of this was Dennis Wheatley's contribution to the Joint Planning Staff (JPS) of the War Cabinet during the Second World War. Wheatley added value to such operations as 'Monty's Double' and 'The Man Who Never Was' and wrote approximately one million words as official papers for the Chiefs of Staff (CoS) to consider in Whitehall. His work was even read by the king himself.

Like Wheatley, Ian Fleming found himself working in Whitehall, but for the Navy Intelligence Department (NID) not the JPS. His call-up to duty was done in the politically correct way of the times: over lunch at the Carlton Grill. He was asked along on 24 May 1939, totally unaware of what was on the military menu that lunchtime; but soon had an inkling when the *Maître d'* showed him to his table. He was met by Rear Admiral John Godfrey and Admiral Aubrey Hugh-Smith.[1] Once introductions had been made, they ordered lunch.

The officers were clearly weighing up the former subaltern from the Black Watch Reserves who had been recommended to Godfrey by Montagu Norman, the Governor of the Bank of England (who had never met Fleming).

If he was of an inquiring mind, Fleming may have known that Admiral Godfrey had been appointed Director of Naval Intelligence (DNI) in February 1939 and, with war looming, was on a recruitment drive.[2] Godfrey had spoken to one of his predecessors, Admiral Sir Reginald Hall, about making a choice of 'right hand man'. During the Great War, Hall had selected a stockbroker as his personal assistant and noted him as invaluable for his tact and skill. He advised Godfrey to do likewise, pointing him towards Montagu Norman (the Governor of the Bank of England), Edward Peacock (head of Barings Bank) and Olaf Hambro (chairman of Hambros Bank), for nominations. It was Norman who would make the recommendation of Fleming and visit Godfrey in person to advise him of his choice.[3] Fleming was a junior partner in the firm Rowe and Pitman,[4] stockbrokers in the city of London, a job he openly disliked.

Godfrey said very little about his plans to Fleming over lunch, content to assess the young man's intelligence instead.[5] He did conclude by stating that Fleming should 'hold himself in readiness for a very special post in time of war'.[6] A few days later, Fleming received the following letter:[7]

> *Sir,*
>
> *I am commanded by my Lords Commissioners of the Admiralty to thank you for the offer of your services to the Admiralty and to inform you that as they would probably*

desire to avail themselves of your offer should hostilities break out, My Lords have given directions that you should be earmarked for service under the Admiralty in the event of emergency.

       I am, Sir,

            Your obedient servant,
            N. Macleod
            Secretary of the Admiralty

Like many cloak and dagger cold war novels, the higher echelons of His Majesties Government during the Second World War was shrouded in old-school networking, fancy lunches and park bench whispers, but for all that, it worked. Shortly after his prestigious lunch at the Carlton Grill, Ian Lancaster Fleming entered Room 39 of the Admiralty for the first time.[8] He started on a part-time basis; but very soon found his feet and became full-time, taking on the rank of lieutenant[9].

Godfrey had worked fast. It is documented that in August 1939 there was only three men within Section 17 of NID:[10] Halahan, Bullock and Fleming. It was admitted that recruitment into the department was 'desperately late but all that DNI had been able to obtain by the time war broke out.'

[11]Fleming quickly immersed himself in the strange and stressful nuances of intelligence work.[12] His covert duties would see him brush shoulders with the enemy and work with real-life war heroes who would inspire him, approximately ten years later, to write the James Bond thrillers that would make him world famous.

This book looks at Ian Fleming's work during the Second World War, the covert operations such as GOLDENEYE (a real operation not just a James Bond fantasy) the intricacies of Operation RUTHLESS (the proposed capture of a German cipher-machine), his covert work in America and the formation of 30 Assault Unit (a crack team of

Commandos in which Fleming played his role). The book is based upon meticulous study of documents in the National Archive (see Annexe A for reference details) and biographical details of the personnel in Fleming's world at that time. It also highlight actual events that Fleming would use to embellish his James Bond novels, such as *Casino Royale.* As you will see, the details were slightly altered in some cases to shroud covert operations, other times they were vastly exaggerated for artistic licence to thrill. This is no criticism because Fleming did not publicise the real counterpart as promotion for the book.

It is important to stress at he outset that Fleming wasn't the real-life James Bond. Also, it is important to state that the real-life military operations Fleming worked on during the war were not the direct inspiration for the James Bond thrillers; although some set pieces were used (as we will discover). That said: it *is* important to learn the intricacies of Ian Fleming's secret war and to understand more about this most popular writer and his work for British Intelligence.

'Any secret service organisation is naturally strange to an outsider . . .'

Airline Detective
Donald Fish

Chapter One

The Real Ian Fleming

'Be true to yourselves. Honesty and integrity are absolutes, but you
will need more. You will need the determination and the courage to
see matters through, even when the fainter hearts have already
taken counsel of their fears. You will need to take hardship, danger,
fatigue and – perhaps above all – uncertainty in your stride . . .
You will need the strength of will and confidence to take the
right road when it is not an easy one.'

Soldier – the autobiography
General Sir Mike Jackson

Ian Lancaster Fleming was born on 28 May 1908 at 27 Green
Street off Park Lane.[13] He was educated at Eton. After a
short period at the Royal Military Academy at Sandhurst,
he went abroad to continue his education. He joined
Reuters News Agency in 1931 after failing to join the
Foreign Office.

During the Second World War, he was personal assistant
to the Director of Naval Intelligence (DNI) and learned
much about covert operations and the intricacies of cipher
messaging. He was also the creator and inspiration of 30
Assault Unit (30 AU), a crack team of commandos who
penetrated enemy territory to gather vital intelligence and
feed it back to NID. After the war he became Foreign
Manager of Kemsley Newspapers and his earliest hardback
book contribution was a chapter in the *Kemsley Manual of*

1

Journalism (Cassell, 1950) concerning the work of a Foreign Correspondent. He published some other miscellaneous articles, but it wasn't until the age of forty-two, on the eve of his marriage, that he wrote the first James Bond novel *Casino Royale* (Jonathan Cape, 1953).

It was in 1957, with the release of the fifth Bond novel *From Russia with Love*, that the series took off and Fleming achieved worldwide fame, some say because President John F Kennedy mentioned *From Russia with Love* was one of his favourite books; others would say that super-stardom would have happened anyway.

Fleming wrote most of his fourteen published James Bond novels/anthologies at Goldeneye, his house in Jamaica. He died of a heart attack on 12 August 1964, aged fifty-six, after suffering a previous heart attack back in 1961. He was buried in the churchyard of Sevenhampton Village, near Swindon.

Authors are often branded aloof, reclusive loners, or embittered elder statesman, who demand respect for their all-too-serious outlook on life. It's a terribly British thing to think; but sometimes that perception is justified. Just to look at images of William Makepeace Thackery or Wilkie Collins would vindicate such thoughts and, unfortunately, the same is true of Ian Fleming.

It is important to acquaint ourselves with the real Ian Fleming before progressing with this book. This book is not a biography but it is biographical writing, so a quick CV and introduction to our main character's personality is needed early on to create the right picture for the reader. So what was Ian Fleming really like?

At the start of his memorial service for the author, William Plomer described Fleming as a man who didn't 'suffer bores gladly' and whose 'curiosity and quick understanding' instilled an 'admiration of what was well done'. This allows us to picture a serious and professional man; some may argue, not dissimilar to his fictitious secret agent James Bond.

Too strong an analogy? For some, not so, as actor Christopher Lee points out,[14] 'in many ways Ian was like Bond. Fiercely intelligent. Athletic ... Women adored him ...'.

Lee is not without family connection. He was Fleming's cousin through marriage. His step-father's sister, Evelyn, was Fleming's mother and to use Lee's words, 'it pleased him [Fleming] to call me his cousin, and it pleased me to return the compliment'.[15]

Lee had a great understanding of Fleming. In the book *The Christopher Lee Filmography*[16] he gives further insight into the author's everyday character, stating: 'Ian was a very sad man, actually. He had everything one could possibly want in a material way, but it wasn't enough. I'm not sure what he wanted – neither was he.'

This perception is enforced by the words of an uncredited person who, during the Second World War, used to share Room 39 with Fleming:[17] 'In a sense he [Fleming] repelled happiness in the innocent forms in which it manifested itself . . . there were moments when quite amusing little remarks were being hurled across the room and Ian was not and had no intention of being "with it". I am not sure there were not moments when one even felt a trifle ashamed of being light-hearted.'

All of these observations are important to our under-standing of Fleming and the way he conducted himself and, ostensibly, his business. He was a serious man, a thinker, a plotter, a cold strategist. Look at his jobs throughout his life: reporter, intelligence officer, stockbroker. Clear thought, rapid response, these were the tools of Fleming's trade. Fleming was a product of his time, sculpted by a traditional education (Eton and, to a smaller degree, Sandhurst) and of the staunch trades he laboured upon and, did a good job at making his own. So I have some sympathy for Fleming's character: Britain made him.

The reminiscences of Fleming highlighted here, shouldn't shock his fans. Popular photographs of the man show him rarely smiling, preferring a staunch stiff-upper-lip pose rather than a happy and relaxed disposition. Fleming wanted to portray the archetypical thinker: hand on chin, elbow on leg.

Robert Harling, a wartime associate of Fleming's, described him as having a 'sad, bony, fateful face', which perhaps enhanced his reputation as a humourless thinker; but you can't help the way you look!

All of this is important information, because it is important to appreciate what some people criticise Fleming for: his coldness. Fleming felt justified when 'the risk of giving offence was nothing compared with the importance of him, if necessary, being blunt'.[18]

History – biography – has not been kind to Ian Fleming. There was a lighter side to his personality, if there wasn't, how on earth could he have written a children's classic such as *Chitty, Chitty, Bang, Bang*? Indeed the two sides of Fleming were qualified to me by Joan Bright, who knew both Ian and his brother Peter during the war: 'I met him when he was in the Admiralty and I was in the Cabinet Office, and somebody said, "Come and have lunch" and that was the way it worked back then. People from different departments would come together . . . We were just friends. We went out for a meal or to the cinema together . . . Ian wasn't the type of man who kept in touch with people. Nothing malicious, he just didn't do it . . . He had a melancholy about him. Quite interesting – if you believe in horrorscopes, which I don't necessarily – we can see by Ian being a Gemini that he had two personalities: the melancholy one and the more humourous one.'

Joan explained that Fleming was a good companion, happy to eat and socialise with people he hardly knew, relaxed when delayed while travelling, 'he would just pull a book out and start reading until we were on our way again'. And also something more, as she is keen to relate: 'I had such a charming letter from him when my husband died. Ian was such a charming man. He would do anything to help me. He was probably cruel to his ladies at times but that's where the duel-personality comes in.'[19]

Fleming was a methodical man. There was a time and a place for everything: good food, good wine, quality golf, a love of writing and, the odd reminiscence about his wartime activity, as again, Christopher Lee is keen to mention (see his autobiography *Lord of Misrule*[20]): 'We talked, not intensely, about cloak-and-dagger operations, he from the eminence of his role as assistant to the Director of Navy Intelligence in the war and I from the chilling experience of working in the aftermath with the Central Registry of War Criminals and security suspects. His mind was dry and cool . . .' Lee goes on to make a comparison between Fleming and James Bond: 'one might wonder if he had ever been shaken and stirred. Like the hero of his thrillers, he could sometimes seem heartless in shrugging away the praise given to able people who had served him well. And he was fourteen years my senior: surveying me quizzically with his cigarette in its tortoiseshell holder set at a slant, he could seem daunting.'

So a professional man, quick minded, agile, a thinker – plotter – clearly with a good capacity for lateral thought. Rarely distracted by humour, conservative in his tastes; always carrying out routine duties the tried and proved way. This isn't just my perception, author Raymond Chandler thought of Fleming in a similar vein: 'Ian Fleming [had a] journalistic mind. I was a journalist once, but . . . I'm too slow a thinker. But Ian – he gather[ed] in every point quickly and accurately.'[21]

So Fleming was just the sort of civilian who would command much respect from the Armed Forces and fitted in well at the Admiralty.

Rear Admiral Godfrey had picked a man with the right attributes for the job. All Fleming had to do now was deliver; and deliver he did.

In March 1940 changes were made to NID that showcase – today – the importance of Fleming within the team; as the following document illustrates:[22]

'Changes in Section 17 JIC work, March 1940

In March, Bullock left and Drake came over from Section 2 to relieve him. Section 17 now consisted of Drake and Halahan, as Staff Officer Intelligence and Staff Officer Operations with Fleming at the centre. The main duties of the two commanders were to co-ordinate intelligence within the Division and to ensure that any of it that affected the other Services or the Foreign Office was passed on and appreciated. At the same time they saw that details of contemplated operations were made available to the appropriate NID country sections. This co-ordination was effected through the Joint Intelligence Committee which met, and continued to meet, daily, and produced appreciations and reports which they considered necessary or which were from time to time called for by the Chiefs of Staff.'

Fleming was at the hub of the new NID, so there is no doubting his influence within it. Mark the fact that this is barely ten months on from his first meeting with Godfrey at the Carlton Grill; and during that period he had been promoted to Commander. Another point worth making is: Fleming had a keen mind and understood much about the covert war effort as time passed on. A great deal of paperwork went across his desk and he made it his job to read all of it and pass the relevant pieces onwards to Godfrey. Fleming would be privy to much intelligence above his rank – because of his relationship with Godfrey – and the impact of this can not be underestimated.

Was all this deliberate on Godfrey's part? To an extent it was. Godfrey needed a man who would be as much in the know as himself and he picked Fleming to be that man. If something happened to him, Fleming would be the continuity man; but many didn't appreciate that.

Within the National Archive at Kew there are thousands of pages of memos and reports stamped Top Secret 'Glint', some written and signed by Fleming (either with full signature, or solely by the letter 'F' (or 17F). There are also other documents referring to Fleming, his ideas and his work, he was certainly a force to be reckoned with, with fingers in many pies.

Although strategically we can not state that Fleming was an enormous influence on the war effort, we can say that he played an enormous part within his department's war effort. This is an important point because there were so many departments within Whitehall that needed rebuilding or creating from grass routes (NID falling into the former category), that each officer within them played an important role in 'bringing the bacon home'. The machinery within every department was finely tuned. Within NID the responsibility for this fell to Godfrey; but if Godfrey was lost, Fleming would pick up the pieces.

Chapter Two

Room 39 and its Players

'Thanks to the valiant of this warlike isle . . .'
Othello – William Shakespeare

Now we understand a little about Fleming himself, let us now look at Room 39 of the Admiralty and the people who worked there. In order to do this effectively, it is important to look at characters that span the whole five years of the war, not just those who were there when Fleming joined. If readers want a more 'point in time' snapshot of NID, then I refer them to Chapter Five where I discuss the distribution of jobs within NID 17 (Fleming's section) at a certain documented moment in time.

First however, let us picture the room: a glorified registry, filled with administrators and naval officers. That's all Fleming's job description was: an administrator for the DNI. Despite the glamorous things associated with him throughout his short career in NID and highlighted in this book (and touched upon in his biographies), let us remain clear: Fleming was recruited as an administer, not to offer ideas and form complex plans (and commando units). A colleague, Donald McLauchlan, explains much about Fleming's formative months in NID: 'he watched such things being organised with the fascination that came to all civilians who found themselves suddenly transferred by war from the brutalities of fiction to the fantasies of fact.'

Perhaps Fleming was at odds with some of the decisions being made by the military personnel above him; but I think not. Fleming wasn't too clear when it came to the protocols of the Royal Navy to begin with and, as such, was a little naive at times. That said, he had the power to stand by his convictions and argue points through with senior officers where perhaps others would back down. He was intelligent enough to know his place, but by remaining cool he could make his thoughts very clear. This amazed some of his colleagues who believed he shouldn't address senior officers, such as the Rear Admiral or First Sea Lord, in such a manner; however McLauchlan observed, 'No one jollied along an obstinate admiral more effectively than Fleming.'

Fleming wasn't a regular officer of the Armed Forces, he held a wartime commission, he had to find his feet in a totally different world and records show that he did so very quickly. Godfrey was extremely impressed with his find and, when one reads the minute sheets of NID files at the National Archive, the brevity and confidence of some of Fleming's comments are nothing but self-assured.

So what environment did Fleming find himself in? Room 39 was a professional environment, as Sefton Delmer[23] described: '[Room 39 was a] vast barn of a room immediately adjoining . . . [the] very comfortable inner sanctum [the rear admiral's office].' The room was sparsely decorated: white walls, an in-use marble fireplace with iron coal-scuttle at its side, with a flimsy gun-metal cabinet beside it. The room had a very high ceiling so, when people spoke loudly, their voices would resonate, almost echo as if in an empty room. Sefton expands upon this, 'A dozen desks of various shapes . . . "clerks" beavered away at stacks of papers. The clerks . . . were all naval officers and their papers were . . . secret reports.' So a hive of activity where slackers would be easily indentified; and Fleming was no slacker, especially when the job fulfilled his dreams of doing something important with his life.

Luxury wasn't the watchword of Whitehall in the 1940s. There were no computers in those days, just an assortment of overworked typewriters; so no virtual registry or database, just papers upon papers and files upon files. Ink, pens, basic filing cabinets with hanging file slings,[24] large black ministry supply telephones constantly ringing; no mobile phones with fancy ring tones. But most unusual of all by today's standards, plumes and plumes of cigarette smoke, mainly coming from the area of the chief clerk's desk – Ian Fleming.

Everybody knew their job. Each desk dealt with radically different intelligence and was given a special code number, Fleming's was 17F.[25]

His desk sat at the window overlooking Horse Guards Parade but more importantly stood guard six feet from the entrance to the Admiral's inner sanctum. Fleming was head boy, ready to counter anyone who dared to enter Godfrey's office.

So what was the Admiral really like? He was the catalyst for much of what Room 39 did, what type of person was he?

Born in Handsworth, Birmingham, July 1888, John Henry Godfrey was educated at King Edward Grammar School, Birmingham, and later Badfield College. He became a naval cadet in 1903, serving on HMS *Britannia*. He rose steadily through the ranks and during the Great War (1916) he was promoted to lieutenant-commander and served in the Mediterranean and Black Sea (1917–1919). He was mentioned in despatches around this time and awarded Légion d'honneur and the Order of the Nile. He was promoted to commander in 1920 and took several desk jobs before being appointed second-in-command of a ship in New Zealand (1925–28). He was promoted to captain on his return and became Deputy Director Staff College (1929–31). After that he commanded HMS *Suffolk* in the China Station (1931–33). He returned as Deputy Director Plans Division (1933–36) and then took command of HMS *Repulse* in the

Mediterranean (1936–38). He then became DNI and rear-admiral from February 1939 and resided in Room 38, behind a green baize door, accessed from Room 39.[26]

So that was the Rear-Admiral's distinguished career up to the war, a man Fleming would spend much time with and, consequently, learn a great deal from. (Although a Rear Admiral I refer to Godfrey as admiral throughout the text, as many people in the civil service utilise this abbreviation). His character was tetchy; some would argue ballsy. He definitely rubbed some people up the wrong way; normally people in other departments. In *Moonraker*, when Bond has a moment of self-analysis, he mentions himself as a commander (which Fleming was himself) RNVSR, 'in his mid-thirties and sitting opposite the admiral'. The admiral being 'M' in the novel; but Godfrey surely in real-life. Godfrey was more M than Fleming was Bond.

So who else shared Room 39 with Fleming?

Captain Charles Drake was essentially the senior officer in the room; but as the work was so varied, nobody assumed command (a very contemporary way of doing things by 1940s standards). Drake, or 'Quaker' as he was sometimes called, had left the services some years previous after a shell exploded in his face. Like Fleming, he too had worked as a stockbroker in the city; but he was a navigator in the Royal Navy and had a wealth of experience, Fleming cultivated his friendship and drew from Drake's experience.

Lieutenant Donald McLauchlan was another man Fleming got on well with. He became the officer in control of navy propaganda, previously he had worked on *The Times* foreign desk (he had spent a short time in their Berlin office).[27] Before that he had been a don at Winchester and was an asset to the Rear-Admiral. Later Fleming would introduce Robert Harling into Room 39, who would become McLachlan's No. 2. In 1965, a year after Fleming's death, McLauchlan described Room 39 in the James Bond tribute book *For Bond Lovers Only*: 'There, about eight or nine strong, sat the personal staff of the Director of Naval Intelligence, Admiral Godfrey. A stockbroker, a lawyer, two captains RN, a paymaster or two, a devoted 'secret lady' and commander Ian Fleming RNVR.'[28]

The 'secret lady' referred to was Patricia 'Paddy' Bennett, who'd worked in NID and the lady who wrote the love letters that would be placed in the pocket of 'The Man Who Never Was'. It is a common belief that the character of Miss Moneypenny in the James Bond novels was based upon Paddy. However, Miss Pettigrew, the private secretary to the head of MI6 is another Moneypenny influence (in an early draft of *Casino Royale*, M's secretary was called Miss Pettavel, or 'Petty'). So again, Bond influences came from various people, not just one, as Fleming always observed when asked.

Robert Harling was a young officer who Sefton Delmer (another member of NID), rather grandly, described as a man who had 'the laughing, big eared, long nosed face of a medieval court jester and the shrewd appraising eyes of a physician.' Not exactly a flattering observation!

Commander Ewan Montagu was another one of Fleming's colleagues. The 'Man Who Never Was' ruse is often acknowledged as Montagu's brainchild. This however, is not so. Montagu wrote the book that became the film *The Man Who Never Was*, but it wasn't his idea.[29] He would, however, win an OBE for his part in the operation and much respect as the author that brought the story to public attention. He didn't get on with Godfrey and left NID to join the Twenty Committee in January 1941.

Another man of note was a young marine called David Astor, who later became editor of *The Observer*. There were certainly a lot of very literate people in Room 39 and very soon, all manner of notable intelligence work was being conducted. Although Fleming hated office work, he began to enjoy NID. With the admiral taking a shine to him he was given greater responsibility. Having completed his 'secretarial' duties, of vetting the overnight intelligence early in the morning and then briefing the admiral, he could construct strategies – set pieces of lateral thought – which could directly counter terrorist attacks on Britain or counter the enemy in Europe. Godfrey would of course be impressed and encourage Fleming to do better. Fleming would later reflect upon his position as a much grander post than it ever was; but that grandness came from the extra contribution he made to the department by making a doddle of his basic job i.e. getting in early enough to do most of it before everyone else got in.

It is true that Fleming over-inflated much of what he did throughout his life, but he was the author of James Bond and a little embroidery here and there added to the drama and intrigue surrounding him. Journalists and fans alike enjoyed the entertainment and he had earned the right to camp it up.

Fleming was not a Walter Mitty character, as the speed in which Admiral Godfrey instated him into the Admiralty indicates, indeed Godfrey said: 'I quickly made up my mind that here was a man for the job, and shortly before the outbreak of the war Fleming was appointed to my staff.'

Although taken on as a lieutenant, he quickly became a commander; Godfrey knew what he wanted from his right hand man; but had to give him the authority to be able to see it through. Fleming worked hard for his rewards though. His typical working day was: arrive at 06.00hrs and go through the previous night's signals. He would then compile sit-reps for the Admiral (who would normally be in office by 08.30hrs). Then he would work through to 13.00hrs, take an extended lunch – sometimes with the Admiral – and then return mid/late afternoon and work through to late evening.

His outwardly professional style complimented with his willingness to work, gave him much responsibility. He also became the filter for all GCHQ correspondence from Blechley Park (where he later got the idea for Operation RUTHLESS) and also the recruitment manager for other RNVR posts within the Admiralty. To some officers, all this wasn't enough. Patrick Dalzel-Job, an officer who later commanded Fleming's crack team of commandos (30 Assault Unit), found him very grey, as he wrote in his autobiography *Arctic Snow to Dust of Normandy:*[30] 'As I know, he never took an active part in 30 AU operations in the field; he appeared once, but did not stay long. However, he directed operations in general terms from the Admiralty and had first sight of our reports, to which he added comments that were pungent and often very amusing. I wish I had had the sense to get copies of the notes he wrote on my submissions'.

Dalzel-Job describes Fleming as an administrator, somebody who could be nothing but desk bound and consequently far removed from the real-life battles of war; he concluded his observations of Fleming by stating: 'someone said that I gave him the germ of the idea of James Bond, but I should think it unlikely.' Is this modesty or disinterest from Dalzel-Job? One gets the impression, the latter. But Dalzel-Job had a dig at NID in his memoirs too, showing his indifference to authority: 'Far too many people in London seemed to be more concerned with the collecting of intelligence for its own sake, than with giving intelligence to those who were able to make use of it.'

This quote from Dalzel-Job illustrate the divide between the administrators and the soldiers,[31] a divide that is still prevalent in the Armed Forces today. A divide that General Sir Mike Jackson so eloquently dug into within his autobiography when reminding his reader of the debt the civilian owes the soldier: 'We are nothing without our soldiers, who deserve the best leadership we can provide. In return, they will respect you, forgive you your inevitable mistakes, and follow you wherever you lead.'

This is all very true; but the average soldier doesn't always understand the political nuances behind certain operations and this causes frustrations. In fairness, he (the soldier) doesn't always need to – in some cases it is good that he doesn't. What Fleming was very good at, was acting as the bridge between the hands and minds of the war effort. He was slap-bang in the middle and had an almost unique position within Whitehall; albeit similar to the role Dennis Wheatley played as a squadron leader (again a wartime commission), 'a conductor of light' rather than the light itself (to paraphrase Sherlock Holmes praise of Dr Watson's powers of deduction). But this is a very important point. It is important to have leaders and soldiers; but it is equally important to have mediators – shapers – people who can think laterally, listen or contribute in a different way but still for the greater good of the 'team'. It sounds all too p.c. for the Second World War maybe, but fascinating that Ian Fleming, like Dennis Wheatley, found this role within Whitehall during the Second World War and was highly praised for his prolific contributions in juxtaposition to the soldiers and leaders.

Perhaps Dalzel-Job was a little too cynical; but then again, so was Bond at times.

'Reading these papers, no one can say that uninstructed imagination, vision, and ability to write attractively are not a great asset if they can be properly harnessed.'

Air Vice Marshal Sir Lawrence Darvell commenting on Dennis Wheatley's war papers, from the Introduction to *Stranger Than Fiction* Dennis Wheatley

Chapter Three

Secret Whitehall

'As we flew eastwards, I wondered what my reception would be
in Whitehall. I didn't fancy that the red carpet would be out;
some form of mat, perhaps.'

The Memoirs of Field-Marshal Montgomery

To look at Whitehall today is to look at Whitehall of
yesterday. Very little has changed on the face of things over
the past sixty years. The old government buildings, from the
Old Admiralty stretching down past the Cabinet Office to 10
Downing Street and then on to the Foreign and
Commonwealth Office (FCO), are the same bricks
and mortar that housed the echelons of the Armed Forces
and the prime minister and his entourage all those years ago.

The ghosts of secrets past echo along darkened corridors,
some unwalked with rooms locked from view for years.
Not just subterranean corridors and tunnels but less covert
below-street level rooms – now dusty and empty – whose
windows stare out at brick walls with metal grills above,
where feet tread every day.

There are routes from the Ministry of Defence (MoD)
Main Building across the busy street – several storeys below
– of Whitehall to other key locations dating back to the
Second World War.

During the bleakest moments of the war, enemy aircraft
and Vengence rockets (V1s and V2s) attacked from above,

but men and women went about their duty in Whitehall bravely, all keen to thwart the Nazi threat. Joan Bright said of the war, 'young people ask me what it was like. They ask if bombs were going off all the time and if I was scared of the V rockets. It's very difficult to say. We all had work to do, one didn't think too much about it at the time.'

The invasion of England was at hand in the early 1940s (Operation Sea Lion), and so many people were afraid that the coming months would unfold the sound of Nazi jack-boots marching down their street. It is easy to look back from the comfortable position of hindsight and marvel at the composure and perception of our forefathers, but unfortunately that is a little removed from the truth. Quite often 'Whitehall' (the prime minister, the war cabinet, advisors, soldiers, agents, scientists) really did not know what they were doing. There was a lot of speculation, a lot of 'sucking it and seeing'. Indeed, at the time of the V2 rockets, the Crossbow Committee didn't know how to stop the height-ening hysteria of the general public, let alone counter the threat of sophisticated rockets with devastating power. The War Cabinet were torn between addressing internal concerns and operational duties – there weren't enough good ideas to go round, let alone people to deal with these ideas. To meticulously plan against the increasing likeli-hood of invasion may seem an incredible thing to contemplate now; but it was so nearly a reality. Somehow the 'talk' (a combination of planning countermeasures and bluff) worked.

In his memoirs Field Marshal Montgomery was not that complimentary about the people who lived and worked in Whitehall. He said that they had no operational know-ledge, which is a little harsh. Many did, but operations in the field were based upon clear first-hand intelligence and a little more spontaneous creativity when implemented than the scenarios devised, discussed, and over-analysed in Whitehall.

Whitehall was a think-tank.

It must be appreciated that naval intelligence, like everywhere else in Whitehall during the war, was filled with logical ideas, keen thought, and all-too-long hours arguing the toss about something that may not happen.

As we have discovered, Fleming was quickly embroiled into the rich web of intelligence work, something he didn't truly understand but, at the same time, fitted nicely into. He could be a good ideas man: the prime minister needed good ideas and the Admiralty was good at producing them, especially when the First Sea Lord Winston Churchill became the prime minister (10 May 1940). But along with these sound ideas creativity was needed and that's where the likes of Ian Fleming and Dennis Wheatley really came into their own.

The phoney war was soon over. Concerning intelligence began to flood in. Maps, maps, maps, were constantly updated with the strategic positions of ships, troops, natural resources. The telephones rang and rang and somebody had to sort the wheat from the chaff, to 'see clearly in the dark', provide lateral thought, perhaps deception and, later, guerrilla strategies to counter the Nazi foe.

Even in the darkness of night, Whitehall failed to sleep. People like Ian Fleming would stay at their desks meditating until late. He would light another cigarette and write his memos, strategies and proposals, mainly to the Admiral, but also to other areas of NID or British Intelligence. It wasn't long before he was given the responsibility to make his own decisions and construct his own real-life scenarios based upon intelligence filtered from Blechley Park or from the Admiral himself. But for all this, this beautiful and romantic picture, it didn't always work. Some intelligence filtered through to Whitehall didn't make it out again, or failed to be transmitted to the right people. There were blunders.

Spike Milligan wrote in part one of his wonderful war

autobiography, *Adolf Hitler, My Part in His Downfall*, 'I never believed that an organization such as ours could ever go to war, let alone win it.' There is truth in comedy and as Spike actually saw active service (fighting at Monte Casino), I sympathise with his perception. By today's standards, the gathering and implementing of military intelligence during the Second World War, was still in its infancy. A lot of lateral thought had to be applied before the blueprint of 'good practice' was laid down. But Whitehall provided that – eventually. People (military and civilians) would learn by their mistakes and work into the night to crystallise their thoughts and shape them into plans. It wasn't one big string of pure brilliant consciousness but rather more a tale of trial and error: the usual toil of human nature.

Fear helped inject urgency. The Battle of Britain began on 10 July 1940. The Luftwaffe's day-time attacks instilled horror and revulsion into the hearts of the British people. But there were the spitfires and hurricanes, so similar on first glance but tactically so different. And that's where Great Britain began to achieve the edge, by subtlety.

'How great a thrill it was for me to make that midnight visit to the War Office can well be imagined, and even more to hear Balfour-Davey's final verdict, which was: "I can't express any opinion on the naval and air matters, but on the military side you have certainly produced a number of ideas that have never occurred to us. And one thing I can promise you. Your paper shall reach VCIGS." (the Vice Chief of the Imperial General Staff.)'

Stranger Than Fiction
Dennis Wheatley

Chapter Four

Operation RUTHLESS

'Well, heaven forgive him! And forgive us all!
Some rise by sin, and some by virtue fall:
Some run from brakes of vice, and answer none;
And some condemned for a fault alone.'

Measure for Measure
William Shakespeare

One of Fleming's early projects at NID was one he devised himself. He learned that the *Kriegsmarine* had a three rotor encoding machine; their own version of the Enigma machine. What Fleming proposed was the arrest of one of the *Kriegsmarine* craft along with a new secret cipher machine and its code book.[32]

Fleming first had to get his idea approved. He presented it to Godfrey, who saw the merits of the operation; this was because Fleming had inadvertently hit a weak point in British naval intelligence with the threat of the new cipher machines. Godfrey approved the operation and assigned Fleming to manage it (a process carried out by the civil service to this day: if you come up with a good idea within your own section, you project manage it yourself and your reputation sinks or swims accordingly).

Operation RUTHLESS was born on 12 September 1940 in a memo Fleming wrote to Godfrey. He explained, by bullet point, his strategy for the operation, which quickly illustrated his foresight for such tasks and explains why he was held in such high regard by the Admiral:

I suggest we obtain the loot by the following means:

1. Obtain from the Air Ministry an air-worthy German bomber.

2. Pick a tough crew of five, including a pilot, W/T [wireless/telegraph] operator and word-perfect German speaker. Dress them in German Air Force uniform, add blood and bandages to suit.

3. Crash plane in the channel after making SOS to rescue service in P/L [plain language].

4. Once aboard rescue boat, shoot German crew, dump overboard, bring rescue boat back to English port.

In order to increase the chance of capturing an R. or M. [Räumboot (small minesweeper); Minenesuchboot (a large minesweeper)] with its richer booty, the crash might be staged in mid-channel. The Germans would presumably employ one of this type for the longer and more hazardous journey.[33]

Fleming added as an afterthought to his document:

N.B. Since attackers will be wearing enemy uniform, they will be liable to be shot as franc-tireurs if captured, and [the] incident might be fruitful field for propaganda. Attackers' story will therefore be 'that it was done for a lark by a group of young hot-heads who thought the war was too tame and wanted to have a go at the Germans. They had stolen plane and equipment and had expected to get into trouble when they got back'. This will prevent suspicions that [the] party was after more valuable booty than a rescue boat.

The head of the Operational Intelligence Centre, Rear Admiral Jock Clayton, gave his support to the RUTHLESS idea and Fleming began to add flesh to the bones of his four point strategy: the bomber would fly before dawn and follow a German air-raid. When it had located a small minesweeper en route, it would cut its engine and drop fast into the water, thus faking a crash.

Let us establish one fact at this point for clarity: cryptologists at GCHQ could read Enigma messages from the German Army and Secret Service, but the *Kriegsmarine* had its own strain of beast, a three rotor encoding machine, which nobody at Bletchley Park could crack. Therefore a *kriegsmarine* had to be acquired along with its codebook and this became the drive of Operation RUTHLESS, as devised by Fleming. Bletchley Park was in full support of the project and offered Fleming as much moral support as they could, especially when he needed to write his memos when constructing the operation.

Frank Birch, head of Naval Section at GCHQ, produced a three page memorandum titled 'Activities of German Naval Units in the Channel', which he presented to Fleming. This was a great help and added even more authority to the project. 'Ruthless' was becoming a reality and that was when Godfrey stepped in to assist:

He acquired a Heinkel 111 bomber through Lord Beaverbrook's office. It had been shot down in a raid over the Firth of Forth and repaired by the Royal Aircraft Establishment, Farnborough. He then sent a man to look through a store of captured enemy equipment (Cardington, Bedford) to acquire some German uniforms.

Fleming leaned back in his chair and watched the implementation of his plan. Smoke curled from his cigarette as he wrote that they needed a 'tough bachelor, able to swim', to head the operation – one cannot help but think of the future Commander James Bond blacking his face and cleaning his PPK ready for action. Little bits of power such as this, i.e.

Fleming being directly involved in covert military activity, were the original seeds of adventure that would fuel the Bond novels.

It was at this point that Fleming volunteered to join the operation himself. Godfrey refused the request on the grounds that Fleming already knew too much about NID to be part of it: he could not possibly fall into enemy hands and face interrogation.

The stage was set, all Fleming had to do now was arrange the players: the crack team that would carry out the operation . . . of which he *wouldn't* be one. But then nothing happened. Why?

There is a memorandum dated 20 October 1940 from Frank Birch[34] it reads:

'Turing [a leading Bletchley Park code breaker] and Twinn came to me like undertakers cheated of a nice corpse two days ago, all in a stew about the cancellation of Operation Ruthless. The burden of their song was the importance of a pinch. Did the authorities realise that, since the Germans did the dirt on their machine on June 1st, there was very little hope, if any, of their deciphering current, or even approximately current, enigma for months and months and months – if ever? Contrariwise, if they got a pinch – even enough to give a clue to one day's material, they could be pretty sure, after an initial delay, of keeping going from day to day from then on; nearly up-to-date if not quite, because the level of traffic now is so much higher and because the machinery has been so much improved. The "initial delay" would be in proportion to the pinch. If the whole bag of tricks was pinched, there'd be no delay at all. They asked me to add – what is self-evident – that they couldn't guarantee that at some future date, near or remote, the Germans mightn't muck their machine about again and necessitate another pinch. There are alternative operations possible. I put up one suggestion myself,

and there are probably lots better. Is there anything in the
wind? I feel there ought to be.'

Fleming's reply to this was that Birch needed to have no fear
that the value of a 'pinch' was underestimated. RUTHLESS
was still fully laid on and the Air Ministry (21 Oct) had
issued elaborate operational orders; they awaited
favourable circumstances but these never transpired.[35]

This information doesn't wholly explain why the
operation was cancelled. Yes, the operation had its critics,
such as Group Captain H.J.Wilson, who was responsible for
captured enemy aircraft. Wilson explained that if the
Heinkel crashed in the sea its Perspex nose cone would be
crushed and the crew would all drown. However, despite
his voice of authority, Wilson lost this argument; as an Air
Ministry document dated 21 October 1940 illustrates: 'Full
Air Ministry Instructions for Operation RUTHLESS:
Official object: to obtain certain important Naval intelligence material known to be carried in German R&M boats,
and certain other types of MTB used on sea security service
and rescue work in the channel.'[36]

So how did it end? Fleming travelled down to Dover
on the 16 October and it was Dover Command that
cancelled the operation solely due to no suitable ships being
in the channel at that time (before 21 October when everybody else was still talking about the operation). That was
the real reason for the disbandment of the project, as a note
from VA Dover to DNI (1029/16 October) reads: 'Operation
RUTHLESS postponed. Two reconnaissance flights by
coastal command revealed no suitable craft operating at
night and evidence from W/T is also negative. Suggest
material and organisation should not be dispersed. Possibly
Portsmouth area may be more fruitful. Lieutenant
Commander [sic] Fleming returned to Admiralty 1800
today Wednesday.'[37]

In summary, Operation RUTHLESS was cancelled due to

some damn rotten – and unforeseen – luck. It would never be reactivated.

Fleming could only lean back in his chair, light another cigarette and dream up a new piece of artistry; but at least he had a blue-print for future operations. RUTHLESS was the ultimate dry run.

Fleming didn't have much luck when it came to the *Kriegsmarine* or, for that matter, German U-boats and their commanders. One, now quite famous story concerning Fleming, was the occasion when he took the captain and navigator of a captured U-boat out to dinner at the downstairs room at Scott's in Covent Garden. His aim: to get them to tell him how they managed to avoid British mines in Skaggerak.

Fleming soon found this a difficult task and the waiter decided to report the table of German speakers to the police.

When Fleming returned to NID he was severely castigated by Admiral Godfrey for activating half of Special Branch at Scotland Yard.

This episode didn't teach Fleming many lessons as he later took officers from the *Bismark* to dinner in order to get them raving drunk and discuss the nuances of their operational duties. On this occasion Sefton Delmer was the first to lose his senses through alcohol and the party all ended up in an MI5 safe house where they prattled on about next to nothing into the wee wee hours of the morning. Suffice to say, not many beans were spilled during these gala occasions.

Chapter Five

The Intricacies of Intelligence

To sit around and dream up fantastic ideas and see some of them come off wasn't what NID was all about.[38] Intelligence had to be gathered, assimilated and acted upon, not just internally but in conjunction with other departments too. NID was a filter to other government departments. The amount of traffic that went through Fleming's desk alone proves that.

As I wrote this book, it was evident that a large part of the 'routine' of NID was missing because I was concentrating solely on Fleming's life. However, to outline what all other sections did – from the charting of U-boats to individual operational requirements is by far and away above the parameters of this book. That said, this chapter takes us a few steps forwards – to 1942 – to show clearly how the 'routine' work in section 17 – Fleming's section – of NID was cut up.[39] As well as who sat on what committee, who was responsible for what and how large the section was.

DUTIES AND STAFF OF SECTION 17, SEPTEMBER 1942[40]

On 11 September 1942, the duties and staff of Section 17 were as follows:

Joint Intelligence Committee work	Capt Baker-Cresswell
	Lt Fletcher-Cooke
	Mr Pell

Joint Intelligence Committee work and Reports	Cdr Drake Daily Situation Cdr Hutchinson Cdr Fleming Lt Cdr Shawcross Mr Pell
Geographical Handbook Section (NID 5) Liaison	Lt Cdr Shawcross Pay-Lt Whitton
Inter-Services Topographical Dept (NID 6) Liaison	Lt Cdr Shawcross Pay-Lt Whitton Lt Foster (NID 2)
Inter-Service Security Board (ISSB)	Cdr Hutchinson Lt Cdr Shawcross Bedford (NID2)
Political Warfare Executive (PWE) Propaganda, Rumours, etc.	Cdr Fleming Lt McLachlan Mr Serpell [possibly Pell]
Special Operations Executive (SOE) (NID 2)	Cdr Squawe Cdr Fleming
Secret Intelligence Service (C)	Cdr Fleming Cdr Drake
Joint Planning Staff (JPS)	Cdr Hutchinson Cdr Drake
Future Planning Section (FPS)	Cdr Hutchinson Lt Cdr Shawcross

Administrative Planning Section (PDQ)	Cdr Hutchinson Lt Cdr Shawcross
Chief of Combined Operations (CCO)	Cdr Hutchinson Cdr Drake Lt Cdr Shawcross
Intelligence Staff Operations (ISO)	Lt Cdr Viscount Dunwich Lt Loudon
Intelligence Planning (plans)	Cdr Drake Cdr Hutchinson
Personal Assistant to DNI	Cdr Fleming
Appt RNVR	Cdr Fleming
Appt Civilian	Mr Merrett

Godfrey had explained to his staff early on that no memos would be distributed that 'argued' with other personnel or their business.[41] That was a waste of paper and energy. All internal conflicts ('bun fights') had to be dealt with in-person and the outcome of those discussions passed on as the 'progress' of each individual task by memo. Also, the mix of personnel within the various tasks (outlined above) ensured greater transparency regarding the intelligence that came into NID and therefore generated a greater pool of personal opinion.

Another point I wish to raise is the relationship between NID and the JPS (the reason for this will become more apparent when I discuss Rudolf Hess in Chapter Eight). It is mentioned in file ADM 223/464 that NID has 'close contact with Joint Planning Staff', also: '[NID] had access to all planning appreciations, reports and memoranda [of the

JPS] and saw copies of the operation orders and signals. It was also NIDs channel of collaboration with the secret organisations – SIS, SOE, PWE and MI5'.

The latter information clearly shows how important NID was to British intelligence work. It had sight of virtually all fundamental documents, minutes and signals to all the major secret agencies.[42] Going back to the JPS, Squadron Leader Dennis Wheatley's boss, Lt Col John Bevan produced a deception plan on 1 August called 'PASSOVER' (the name was afterwards changed to 'OVERTHROW') designed to retain the enemy in Western Europe with a cover plan called 'SOLO' (CoS approved these deceptions on 8 August).

It is interesting that two of the most popular writers of the twentieth century worked so closely together during the Second World War: thriller writer Ian Fleming and occult/adventure novelist Dennis Wheatley. Indeed, Wheatley knew Ian through Peter Fleming and they sometimes dined together.

We will return to this friendship again, but it does give another indication as to why deception plans were considered by NID – because of that 'special relationship' with JPS, nurtured by Fleming and Wheatley.

'In August, while the Battle of Britain raged overhead, the JPS were already considering some of the problems concerning the grim winter that lay before us. The RAF was already committed to the limit, there was little that the Navy could do on its own, and all the Army in Britain could do, as new supplies of weapons came forward, was to train with the utmost intensity to resist the invasion we were all expecting, if not within a matter of weeks, then certainly in the coming spring.'

Stranger Than Fiction
Dennis Wheatley

Chapter Six

Taking Life Seriously

'I shall act not in a rash or hasty manner,
and on which I give you my word of honour.'

Lord Nelson

It was in 1940 that Fleming and Godfrey contacted Professor of Geography, Kenneth Mason, at Oxford University.[43] They were keen to prepare in-depth reports devoted to the physical geography of countries engaged in military operations.[44]

These intelligence reports became the precursor for the Naval Intelligence Division Geographical Handbook Series (1941–46) which grew steadily through intelligence reports – instigated by Fleming and Godfrey – in 1940.

It is extremely important not to underestimate the importance of these early documents and how they progressed into handbooks, as the Armed Forces as a whole would come to rely upon them for operational needs. The intelligence and clear geographical facts collated by Fleming enhanced the reputation of NID across the Armed Forces. This work was one of the most significant things Fleming did in naval intelligence; it certainly paved the way for the work he did with 30AU, albeit in ground-work terms.

It has been suggested that intelligence for the reports (and later handbooks) was collated by NID from Bletchley Park and the geographical facts from Oxford and

Cambridge scholars. But the fact remains, Godfrey and Fleming were the first to bring these disparate groups together to create a fuller – clearer – picture of specific countries. The resulting wide-spread use of the literature vindicates the praise extended to NID for their ultimate product.

Let us briefly examine Fleming's relationship with Bletchley Park, as it seems to be somewhat ill-defined.

Firstly, he was never 'on the staff' there as sometimes claimed. He was a point of contact within NID for Bletchley Park and therefore privy to much of what went on there: he never resided there. Bletchley Park was, from August 1939, the Government Code and Cipher School (sometimes referred to as Golf, Cheese and Chess Society). It also went under the name 'Station X'; not to be confused with 'Camp X', Whitby, Ontario, where Fleming was rumoured to have visited in the past.[45]

Was NID always a respected store room for intelligence and did it always share that important information with the right people at the right time? No it didn't and perhaps the most damning criticism comes from none other than Patrick Dalzel-Job, of 30 AU. In his autobiography *Arctic Snow to Dust of Norway*, Darzel-Job explained that vital information given to NID from SIS field agents, 'was locked away in the most secret places in the British Admiralty, and could not be communicated'. He further commented that intelligence officers were over keen and collected all sorts of useless facts to the extent where they 'couldn't see the wood from the trees.'

This was not new criticism of intelligence gatherers, as T E Lawrence mentions in *Seven Pillars of Wisdom*: 'such haphazard playing with the men and movements of which we had assumed the leadership disgraced our minds. I vowed to know henceforward, before I moved, where I was going and by what roads.'

Dalzel-Job also mentioned that he and others had given detailed maps of the waters around Norway to NID before and during the war, maps that were essential to plotting strategies against the Nazis, but these maps were lost – only to be found years later stuck behind a cabinet.

It is almost as if Godfrey and Fleming knew their shortcomings and decided to do something positive about it through the Naval Intelligence Division Geographical Handbook Series.

The NID Handbook series was the positive step adopted to address, in a methodical way, all the intelligence that was coming into the Admiralty from various sources and countries (and filtered through many of the meetings attended by NID 17, as detailed in Chapter Five). Once collated, analysed and put into context in individual volumes, criticisms, like the one made by Dalzel-Job, became less frequent.

There is much talk of the unprofessional way Whitehall conducted certain business during the war. Organised chaos seems to be a good description of the day-to-day struggle to stay one step in front of the enemy and prevent the public from panicing (especially when the V rockets began to fall). Countermeasures, plans, strategies, propaganda, deceptions had to be put in place so quickly and not all of them were successful; but they were all based upon logical – good quality – ideas.

Gathering intelligence against the Nazis wasn't a new thing, it didn't start as soon as war was declared on Germany. It had been going on seamlessly since the end of the Great War. However, more 'concern' and more quality intelligence was gathered from the moment Adolf Hitler brought 'professional' groups of soldiers together; not just the SS but the German foot-soldier as well. These groups were such professional entities and this gave great cause for concern.[46]

To an extent, intelligence gathering became a whole new ball game, especially in comparison to previous conflicts: because of the immediate use of the intelligence gathered and the high importance of quick assimilation and action (to implement countermeasures).

This became Whitehall's major task through the JPS, NID and the SIS.

'I instructed Callistus that the cipher-like communications between departments must cease and correct Latin or Greek longhand be substituted: the new officials must be allowed to understand what was going on.'

Claudius the God
Robert Graves

Chapter Seven

Operation GOLDENEYE

'No man is born a hero.
To believe such would be pretentious conceit;
nor is heroism shallow vanity or self-glorification.'

Unsung Heroes
Erik Durschmied

Perhaps the most talked about aspect of Ian Fleming's secret war today is Operation GOLDENEYE. This work has become somewhat iconic for two reasons: one, it was the name Fleming would give his house in Jamaica in the late 1940s and two, it became the name of a popular James Bond movie starring Pierce Brosnan (which was not actually based upon a Bond story written by Ian Fleming).

Apart from these two unrelated incidents there is no major reason why this operation should require more fame than any other aspect of Fleming's war. Operation GOLDENEYE was *not* the basic plot to a James Bond thriller and not, as it turned out, of any long-term significance to the British Armed Forces or their operational strategies. What it was however, was a good intelligence exercise for Fleming, something he could nurture and manage from start to finish.

Operation GOLDENEYE would earn Fleming many plaudits, even though it didn't need to be activated. Fleming had constructed the operation to Godfrey's specifications and the Admiral was happy with Commander Fleming's work.

So what was Operation GOLDENEYE?

It was a plan to monitor Franco's Spain and its possible alliance with the Axis Powers. It also incorporated plans to defend Gibraltar if the Germans invaded through Spain. Gibraltar was – and had been since at least Lord Nelson's time – a major strategic position for British ships in the Mediterranean and, naturally, the Royal Navy were concerned that it could be taken away from them[47].

Although Godfrey gave Operation GOLDENEYE to Fleming, he was not exactly resting on his laurels. He would take on Operation TRACER single-handedly, which went hand-in-glove with Operation GOLDENEYE.[48] Fleming also arranged for the military attache's job in Madrid to be upgraded and given to a good friend of his, Captain Alan Hillgarth.[49] The captain had successfully evacuated British subjects in Majorca in 1938 via HMS *Repulse*, where Godfrey was commanding officer. [50]

Fleming also appreciated the historical importance of 'the Rock' as he was a keen Nelson enthusiast. He would bury himself deep into the work in-hand as England expected.

Fleming was issued with a temporary passport and on 16 February 1941 he flew out to Gibraltar to instigate the practical side of Operation GOLDENEYE. He would begin by monitoring the military installations in the Mediterranean; how they worked, the traffic, cargo, military usage. Lots of consideration was given to 'refuge ports for Spanish, Portugese and neutral merchant ships.' Fleming had to grasp how the nautical side of the Mediterranean worked, only then could he explore how British and allied shipping would work if Gibraltar was knocked out of the equation. Once he had a grip on this he returned to Madrid to discuss his findings with Captain Hillgarth.

One thing Hillgarth was very interested in was Fleming's meeting with William Joseph Donovan, an officer from the American Office of Strategic Services. The Allies were a major source of strategic back-up and it was important that they were kept abreast of British plans and incorporated into them in the most productive way.

Fleming had discussed the Nazi threat in the Med' and both the British and the Americans had a vested interest in keeping the Nazis at bay. He went on to discuss the loan of US destroyers for leases to British Atlantic bases.

Fleming returned to London via Lisbon on 26 February to report to Godfrey, who was keen to hear first hand what Fleming had achieved, mainly to assist the intricacies of his own – covert to many within NID – Operation TRACER.

The commander RNVR was a little cautious in his wording to begin with. There had been so much to take in, assimilate and then, to negotiate. Judging by the strained way he spoke about this trip years later, Fleming may have felt that he should have done more to move things forward at the time.

Before we move on to Godfrey's Operation TRACER, let us understand Hillgarth's problem with Operation GOLDENEYE. Fleming appeared to like Hillgarth but Hilgarth did have some concerns regarding Fleming's work.

Captain Hillgarth's note (subject: Goldeneye, dated 20.11.41) praised Fleming, he had clearly liaised with the right people, it was now simply a case of nurturing relationships up to the moment of invasion. People needed to be kept on-side and this was the important on-going factor. Hillgarth wrote: 'Goldeneye is really a precaution against a German invasion of Spain. It was designed to provide personnel and means of communication for a small Naval mission to the Spanish Navy, and the fact that no invasion has yet taken place does not justify any relaxation.'

Hillgarth went on to say that the naval side of the

operation (originally tri-service) was 'unnecessarily ambitious'. He proposed to step down many officers who were part of the current obligation, because the same outcome could be achieved with fewer staff. Perhaps Fleming's plans were a little too elaborate; but in his defence, this was an opportunity to be grasped because of the strategic importance of Gibraltar.

Despite Hillgarth's criticism, Fleming was not castigated. He had done a good job at putting things in place, the fact that the threat had eventually gone away was immaterial. Fleming had showed great self-reliance and motivation with Operation GOLDENEYE, leaving the admiral to concentrate on other important issues. This in itself was commendable.

Although one could suggest that a second operation had now gone pear-shaped for Fleming, Godfrey didn't see it that way; quite frankly, it was a good thing GOLDENEYE didn't have to happen. Not because there was anything wrong with Fleming's work but because of the hassle and cost to resources and lives. War should be avoided but countermeasures had to be put into place if war was necessary.

That's right, countermeasures, not countermeasure: Godfrey's Operation TRACER ran parallel to Operation GOLDENEYE. It has never been proved that Fleming had any dealings with this exercise. Godfrey dealt with the bulk of the work connected with this operation at home in Mayfair and Fleming made no comment about it during his lifetime, either because: one, the work was deemed too secret up to Fleming's death or two, he didn't have any part in it. I think the latter.

Operation TRACER was a mission to seal six volunteers inside the Rock of Gibraltar if it was captured by the Nazis. From inside 'the Rock' the team could monitor enemy movements through two twelve inch by six inch slits; one looking east and one looking west. An eighteen foot radio antenna was to be thrown out of one of the observation slits to enable the operators to radio details of enemy targets to the RAF. The cavern was to be forty-five foot by eighteen foot wide and eight foot high. They were to be given food and water supplies (some say for seven years; other say for a more realistic one year).

Volunteers were told that they would be sealed in with no possible way out. If they died they would have to be embalmed and cemented into the walls by the survivors.

At his home in Mayfair, Godfrey held secret meetings with Murray Levick, who was part of Captain Scott's last expedition to the Antarctic (by now in his mid sixties). Godfrey asked the surgeon-commander pertinent questions to do with survival techniques based upon his experiences: questions about diet, sanitation, rations (including alcohol and tobacco), along with the nuances of the more psychological aspects of the operation. It was then planned that training for the operation would take place in Scotland. Levick agreed to come out of retirement to assist Godfrey in organising the whole operation. He would also be the main interface.

Volunteers were taken from the naval school at Shortley, Suffolk, for training before being sent to Gibraltar under separate job descriptions. One of these volunteers was Surgeon Lieutenant (RNVR) Dr Bruce Cooper.[51]

The volunteers were given radio training by Brigadier Gambier-Parry, the MI6 expert in radio techniques, who provided them with special equipment and a bicycle-operated generator.

Godfrey was so enthused by the project, he believed similar TRACER operations should be set up in Colombo, Trincomalee, Malta and Aden.

The operation was closed down in August 1943, when the threat of Nazi invasion was lessened.

Godfrey was still insistent that TRACER sections should

be prepared around the world in case of future wartime requirements. A manual was provided, giving details of how TRACER should operate. This included details about food, cooking, equipment, clothing, games, surgical instruments, stationery; even what books one should read![52]

Whitehall took these islands extremely seriously and several operations were built up to thwart the prospect of invasion. They were only put to one side – not cancelled – when the Franco/Nazi threat of invasion went away).

Operation TRACER may seem by today's standards a naive attempt at gathering intelligence during occupation; but it does highlight some of the concerns of the period.

Aside from Operations GOLDENEYE and TRACER, there were others that existed concerning Gibraltar. Part of Operation TORCH activities was a 'Gibraltar Cover Plan'. This was activated very early on in the TORCH campaign. Its aim was to discount the mounting activity at Gibraltar by suggesting that the relief of Malta was at hand. David Strangeways, from the Duke of Wellington's Regiment, was sent to Gibraltar by John Bevan with an 'indiscreetly' signed copy of Dennis Wheatley's latest novel for a gentleman by the name of Henry Hopkins. The plan was that luggage would be checked by Axis agents while in Gibraltar – even the governor was in on the deception.

Indeed, much time was taken in securing Gibraltar as a decoy tool as well as a strategic base.

Chapter Eight

Flight of Fancy

'My personal view is that he has lost favour and in order to
rehabilitate himself he has cunningly conceived the idea of
appearing as a Peace Envoy to enable him to justify his action . . .'
Report on Rudolf Hess by Major Sheppard, 21 May 1941

The astonishing flight of Rudolf Hess from Augsburg to
Scotland on 10 May 1941 is one of the great mysteries of the
Second World War. Why did he make the trip? Was it to
negotiate peace between Britain and Germany? Was it a
crude attempt at recruiting fifth columnists to support an
invasion of Britain? Could it be both these things? More
importantly, what role did British intelligence and Ian
Fleming play in this strange episode?

Despite the amount of literature written about Rudolf
Hess' last flight and the amount of official records studied,
nobody has satisfied the public's longing as to why Hess
flew to the UK.[53] Perhaps the true answer isn't satisfying
enough. Perhaps people are searching for an explosive
reason when, in actual fact, there isn't one.

Many conspiracy theorists claim that Fleming organised
Hess' trip: that he framed Hess into believing that there was
a group of anti-Churchill activists in Britain who wanted to
overthrow the government. This story isn't without some
truth. Fleming definitely had an interest in Hess' trip, but
just how much was Fleming involved?

What has added to the cauldron of conspiracy is Peter Fleming's novel *The Flying Visit*, which was written shortly before Hess' flight and gave a fictional account of Adolf Hitler's unexpected arrival in Britain during an air raid after his aircraft had been shot down![54] For the deputy führer to crash-land approximately a year after the release of that light-hearted novel made people wonder about Peter Fleming's prophetic gifts – or his inside knowledge![55]

In order to make some clear statements about the Flemings' association with the Rudolf Hess story, we first need to ascertain the facts – as we know them – of Hess' trip. We then need to discover the intelligence-feed at the time and how Ian and Peter were worked into that mix. To begin with, the facts concerning Hess's flight:

Rudolf Hess parachuted from his Messerschmitt BF110 (works number 3869) and landed at Floors Farm, west of Eaglesham in Renfrewshire in May 1941. His aircraft crashed nearby and he was quickly taken into custody, initially giving the alias of Hauptmann Alfred Horn, he explained that he had an important message for the Duke of Hamilton.

Little did Hess know that Hamilton had been following the Nazi's progress over Britain on the plotting board, followed by three Hurricanes from the newly formed 317 (Polish) Squadron. Later, Hamilton received a phone call from his old colleague of 602 Squadron, Hector MacLean. It was not clear at that time who the German pilot was; as the conversation implies:

> *'What's all this about, Hector?'*
> *'A German captain has parachuted from a Me110 and wants to see you.'*
> *'Good heavens, what does he want to see me about?'*
> *'I don't know, he won't say.'*
> *'What do you think I should do about it?'*
> *'I think you should go and see him.'*
> *'Yes, I think I will.'*[56]

The rest of Hamilton's involvement can be best explained in the words of His Grace the 15th Duke of Hamilton:

> *'As a real part of Hamilton's life, the Hess episode was little more than a five day wonder. When Hess landed he gave a false name to everybody and asked to see the Duke of Hamilton. Hamilton saw him, and Hess then revealed his real identity and the purpose of his mission. Hamilton thereafter saw him twice more in the presence of Ivor Kirkpatrick, the British Foreign Office expert on Germany. That was the limit of his direct contact with Hess, all three occasions taking place during one week in May 1941.'*

It is important to make Hamilton's position clear, as many conspiracy theorists have argued that he had met Hess before the war in Germany, something which has been fiercely denied by the Hamilton estate.[57]

So now let us consider two other important points: one, Hess's motives for flying to Scotland to see the duke, and two, the role of British intelligence, including the Flemings, in the Hess story (before and after the flight).

Hess wanted to meet the Duke of Hamilton and the very fact that he introduced himself to Hamilton by his real name implies that he believed that Hamilton would welcome him but Hamilton knew nothing about it: Hess had been duped lock, stock and barrel. So much so, he went on to tell Hamilton that he had seen him at the Berlin Olympic Games in 1936, as a point of significance. This cut no ice with Hamilton as *he* hadn't knowingly seen Hess. But Hess believed it; perhaps through some correspondence he believed came from Hamilton (which had really come from British intelligence).

Hess explained that Hitler didn't want to defeat Britain and hoped to stop the fighting. (My guess is that this wasn't said so flatly.) He may have skipped around such words, as

Adolf Hitler didn't even know that Hess had gone to Scotland!

Hess went on to explain that he had tried to arrange a meeting with Hamilton in Lisbon, via Albrecht Haushofer,[58] and had also made three previous attempts at reaching Britain (which was true).[59]

Haushofer had written to the Duke of Hamilton on 23 September 1940; Haushofer sent the letter via Lisbon, requesting that they meet there but this letter never reached Hamilton. It was intercepted by MI5 and Hamilton wasn't shown it, or even told of its existence until Hess had arrived. What did MI5/British intelligence do about that letter? Did they just sit on it? Surely not! Were they making enquiries into Hamilton's character? Probably not; but why hold the letter?

We are fairly sure that Hess wanted Hamilton to talk to his political party and arrange peace talks; he had no desire to make contact with an underground group of fifth columnists.

Also, Hess soon wanted Hamilton to arrange a 'parole' via the king as he had flown to Britain unarmed and of his own free will, which suggests that he had a clear objective in coming to UK.

Hess had put much faith into his flight and, more importantly, his 'personal contact' in UK. This was probably because Haushofer had suggested contacting Hamilton in the first place. Hess trusted Haushofer. There was history between the two men; Haushofer had allegedly developed some kind of friendship with Hamilton just prior to the outbreak of the war. Hess then received a letter from British intelligence that convinced him that Hamilton had noticed him at the Olympics . British intelligence didn't mention any of this to Hamilton and possibly replied to Hess as 'a bit of fun', not truly suspecting that anything would come of it. Either that or they kept it all to themselves to begin with as a special top secret deception plan; but who was responsible?

Hess was quite a naive man, because when Hamilton actually met him it quickly became clear to the duke that Hess didn't know much about the British political system. Surely any top Nazi flying to UK would acquaint themselves with such things before flying? In short, Hamilton could do little to help Hess. Hess was put into custody where he suddenly began to suffer from amnesia – he was a broken man from then on.

> 'Rudolf Hess was the odd-man-out at Nuremberg . . . His only systematic interrogation took place in Britain in the early summer of 1941, following his flight to Scotland. These interviews showed that Hess was the victim of a profound delusion about the nature of British politics and society. He had expected an official reception and the chance to talk peace; instead he was treated first as a criminal, then, following his transfer to a secure location in Wales, as a mental patient.'
>
> *Interrogations, the Nazi Elite in Allied Hands, 1945*
> Richard Overy

Let us now look more closely at point two and discuss British intelligences' stance with regard to this matter.

Hamilton immediately tried to call the permanent secretary of the Foreign Office (FO), Sir Alexander Cadogen, to organise an appointment. Jock Colville,[60] the prime minister's private secretary, took the call and told Hamilton that he had just arrived and knew about Hess. He also wanted to know what Hamilton proposed to do about it. Colville then organised a meeting between Hamilton and the prime minister for later that day; Churchill seemed more interested in watching *Go West*, the new Marx Brothers movie, after dinner than hear too much more about the Nazi, 'Hess or no Hess, I am going to see the Marx Brothers,' he is quoted as saying.[61]

The important player in this part of this story is Colville, who had been reading Peter Fleming's *The Flying Visit* [62] at the time. Colville also knew that there was a belief that Hitler might be sky-jacked and flown to RAF Lympne, Kent, by his private pilot, Hans Bauer, who was unhappy with Germany's conduct during the war. This intelligence had come from the British Air Attache in Bulgaria, and plans had been made to receive the Führer at Lympne. Colville later wrote in his autobiography *The Fringes of Power*, 'I felt sure that either Hitler or Goering had arrived.' Colville believed the Nazi could possibly have been Goering because of his proposed visit to Britain in late August 1939. [63]

So what does this tell us about Peter Fleming's involvement? Did he have sight of Albrecht Haushofer's letter and more importantly have a hand in replying? [64] One would say, unlikely; but can it be ruled out?

What about the SOE? Were they involved?

The Special Operations Executive (SOE), aka The Baker Street Irregulars, was set up by Winston Churchill and Hugh Dalton in July 1940. This gave Godfrey some breathing space as field work executed by NID would transfer to SOE.

The SOE was formed from three other departments, namely Section D (SIS) commanded by Major Lawrence Grand, Military Intelligence Research (MI R) headed by Major J C Holland, and Department EH (a propaganda department in Electra House) run by Sir Campbell Stewart. The propaganda department would later break away from the SOE to form the Political Warfare Executive (PWE).

SOEs main aim was to 'facilitate espionage and sabotage behind enemy lines' and serve as the nucleus of a resistance unit if Britain was invaded by the Axis Powers. The SOE was dissolved officially in 1946, with much of its ongoing work reverting to MI6. [65]

It is speculated in some quarters that Violet Roberts, whose nephew was a relative of the Duke of Hamilton working in political intelligence and propaganda (SIS), was friends with Haushofer and wrote him a letter, which Hess found fascinating. I cannot substantiate such claims unfortunately.

Edvard Beneš, head of Czechoslovak Government in Exile (and his intelligence chief František Moravec, who worked for SOL/PWE) speculated that British intelligence used Haushofer's reply to Violet Roberts as a means to trap Hess.

There is a strange lack of checkable documentation between the original letter to Hamilton and Hess landing; it's much a case of what the archive doesn't say rather than what it does say. If anything the Czechs supported the idea of British intelligence involvement.

SOE and NID were closely associated with each other at the time of Hess's flight and Fleming would have learned very quickly about Hess (because he saw much intelligence from a variety of sources). We know for certain that Fleming tracked down Aleister Crowley for advice concerning Hess's interrogation, which prompted Crowley to write to DNI. But why on earth would Fleming do that? Crowley had been dubbed the wickedest man in the world, a master of the Black Mass, who once apparently summoned Pan and was left a jibbering wreck. Although still a master of the Occult and Astrology during the Second World War, Crowley was more content to write propaganda poems than summoning up ancient demons; but he did write to Godfrey, the sealed letter covered in occultist symbols. The letter read:

> Sir:
>
> If it is true that Herr Hess is much influenced by astrology and magick, my services might be of use to the Department in case he should not be willing to do what you wish. I have the honour to be, sir,
>
> > Your obedient servant
> > Aleister Crowley[66]

Included with the letter was one of Crowley's poems entitled 'England Stand Fast'.

Crowley's offer of support was rejected by DNI and no more was said on the matter; but what made Fleming suggest Crowley in the first place?

Apparently, the night after Hess' historic flight to Scotland, there was a rare alignment of six planets in the astrological sign of Taurus. Some believe that Hess felt that this would greatly increase his chances of a successful operation, as he was deeply interested in astrology. Did Fleming know this and alert Crowley?

In *The Man Who Was M: The Life of Charles Henry Maxwell Knight*, Anthony Masters goes as far as to claim that Fleming was the intelligence officer behind the Hess flight. He explains that a trap was laid in 1940, after Fleming read about the anglo-German organisation 'the Link'[67] in the intelligence files of Sir Barry Domvile. Then via an agent, Fleming fed Hess the line that 'the Link' had been driven underground and was in a position to overthrow the prime minister and negotiate peace.[68] He was also told that the Duke of Hamilton was prepared to be a negotiator.

The whole ruse wasn't something Godfrey was in on because he rejected Crowley at the time of interrogation. But if he was, one could argue that the operation was already complete at the time of rejection, Hess captured and nothing more needed to be done. A cover up was then much more important; as questions concerning the Duke of Hamilton and Hess were being asked in the House.

It makes a lot of sense to suggest that British intelligence was involved somewhere along the line and they tricked Hess into flying to UK. If they were behind it, then who? There is documented evidence to suggest that the SOE tried to arrange a plot against Hitler in late 1944, part of Operation FOXLEY. The sequel to this, a plot against Himmler, would include Hess as an assassin (this is mentioned in a memo dated 18 December 1944 under X Plans.[69])

Although nothing came of these plans, the idea shows that Hess was in SOEs thoughts. So British intelligence do get themselves involved in this story in a bit of a dramatic way, taking advantage of circumstances and using Hess as bait in their own plans.

What about other government offices such as The Double Cross Committee? This was a group also known as the Twenty Committee (so called because the Roman numerals, XX, formed a double cross). Again, Fleming and others (such as the former NID officer Ewan Montagu) were known to each other.

Due to a combination of counter-espionage work prior to the war and signals intelligence during it, MI5 were in a position to monitor and pick up German agents who were 'dropped' into Britain. In short, British intelligence had the power to covertly lure Hess to UK: perhaps after some discussion a letter was generated to Hess/Albrecht? It was a chancer's daydream but British intelligence had nothing to lose. The very fact that they hadn't informed Hamilton of the letter in the first place may suggest that they half-thought that Hamilton had some connection with Hess. Maybe they wanted to hedge their bets even though the prospect was unlikely? Much more plausible is the idea that their reply would mount to nothing so the whole thing should be forgotten about.

'I am not particularly interested in having my fortune told, but I am rather interested by fortune-telling and all matters connected with extra-sensory perception.'

Thrilling Cities
Ian Fleming

One of the last photographs of Rudolf Hess in Spandau has him pictured with detailed maps of the moon. These are pinned to the wall of his cell directly above his bed. Also the character of Le Chiffre in the James Bond novel *Casino Royale* is based physically on Aleister Crowley; just as the evil occultist in Dennis Wheatley's *The Devil Rides Out* is based upon Crowley.

Wheatley was working down the road from Fleming in the Cabinet War Rooms. Wheatley had already met Crowley in the early 1930s. Peter Fleming was a member of the London Controlling Section (LCS), which Wheatley was a member of, but they were also very good friends too. And the LCSs remit was to gather psychological warfare strategies into the intelligence services (Wheatley solely working on deception plans). Did two of the greatest writers of the twentieth century come together to lure Rudolf Hess to the UK meeting through Peter Fleming? Did Fleming contact Wheatley and through him get Crowley's contact details? Both Fleming and Wheatley would have connections with all other departments including the Twenty Committee, so therefore could call on people when need-be.[70]

We can now add into this mix Lois de Wohl, an astrologer who had worked for NID in charting the exact moments when Hitler might be susceptible to deception.

Mr De Wohl suggested:

Hitler regards the good and bad aspects of his horoscope as the factors of good and bad luck. When he is up against odds, he will wait until the aspects are good. That is why he waited from Oct 1939 to April 1940 before invading Norway and Denmark.

The practical purpose of his report, said Mr de Wohl, was to find out when Hitler was likely to undertake major action, and, secondly, what periods, regarded by him as unlucky, were suitable for attacks upon him. Mr De Wohl proceeded to an elaborate astrological analysis, month by month, expressed in astrological terms and in plain language. His general conclusions were that Hitler would be unlucky between Sep 16, 1940 and October 19, 1940; March 8th, 1941-April 10th, 1941; April 18th, 1941–May 5th, 1941[71]; and that his period of luck was from the end of October 1940 until the end of the first week of March.

Perhaps Hess was also being analysed by NID and, was successfully lured to UK through a combination of Wheatley, de Wohl and Crowley, neatly brought together by the Flemings over lunch or a stimulating conversation over dinner?

It is my belief that Wheatley only provided the link with Crowley, whilst Fleming dreamed up the idea in the first place. It is a matter for conjecture but my main points are: we know Fleming contacted Crowley. Why? How? Logically through the only person he knew who knew him: Dennis Wheatley. We also know Wheatley knew Crowley and had knowledge of the occult because of his much publicised audiences with him while researching *The Devil Rides Out*. Finally we know the Nazis, especially Hitler and Hess, had an interest in astrology (which was something Wheatley exploited in his fiction *They Used Dark Forces*) and this was taken seriously by British intelligence in their use of de Wohl. This is something worthy of further investigation, especially as, very soon after Hess' crash, Godfrey and Fleming left for America; was this to allow things to calm down? Thaddeus Holt suggests that the main reason for Godfrey going to America was to discuss the work of a double agent code-named Tricycle.[72] It is possible that Godfrey had meetings with this man, while Fleming got on with other things.

'There are, of course, plenty of well-authenticated accounts of those terrible last days in Berlin; Goering's dismissal, Himmler's treachery and Hitler's savage attempt to involve the whole German people in his own ruin; but although faith he placed in astrologers is well known, no one has yet described how his belief in supernatural guidance influenced his final decisions.'

They Used Dark Forces
Dennis Wheatley

There is an interesting document nestling in FO 371 within the National Archive. It presents a seven point list of facts connected with the Hess flight. It runs as follows:

i) Hess first approached Haushofer (with or without the knowledge of Hitler) on 8 September 1940 regarding the chances of an anglo-German peace. Among other possibilities, the 'Hamilton Plan' was here first mentioned.

ii) On the strength of this, Hess wrote on 10 September 1940 (this letter is not available) to Haushofer stating preference for the 'Hamilton Plan'.

iii) In reply to (2) Haushofer wrote on 19 September 1940 to Hess, expressing sceptism of the chance of anglo-German peace, yet nevertheless sketching 'modus operandi' for the 'Hamilton Plan'.

iv) It is clear that Haushofer wrote to the Duke of Hamilton at the end of September 1940, via Lisbon, and received no reply.

v) In April 1941, Haushofer was approached by Burckhardt, vice president of the international Red Cross, whom, soon afterwards and with Hess' approval, he met in Genova and who allegedly spoke of an important person from London who was anxious to talk peace with the Germans, Haushofer promised to return to Genova if this person's intention was serious.

vi) Meanwhile – it can only be surmised – the 'Hamilton Plan' continued to obsess the mind of Hess, until, with or without further recourse to Haushofer, he resolved to carry out the mission himself and, Mahomet-like, to 'go to the mountain', since clearly 'the mountain' would not come to him – or even meet him half way.

vii) Immediately on the discovery of Hess' departure, Hitler sent for Haushofer, as being the person virtually responsible for the plan which Hess had adopted and put into practice in so unorthodox a manner.

[this is confirmed in a cipher from Mr Kelly 29 July 1941 to FO]

Bullet five is very interesting; because no one can say who the 'important person from London' really was.

Strangely, I do believe that Winston Churchill and other senior officers were convinced that Hess flew to UK of his own accord. There is so much documented evidence on this fact alone. I don't believe in any kind of conspiracy theory; just one of the best con tricks of the Second World War. Let me leave you with these thoughts:

i) If you were the deputy Führer would you admit to being duped so badly (maybe insanity was the easy way out)?

ii) If you had planned the whole escapade on the off chance and then suddenly found it had come off but questions were being asked in the House, would you admit to the ruse?

'He [Hess] was almost certainly genuine in his belief that peace could be negotiated and his beloved Fuehrer saved from the folly of a two-front war.'
Interrogations – the Nazi Elite in Allied Hands, 1945
Richard Overy

Chapter Nine

The Future of USA Intelligence

It was 25 May 1941 when Fleming and Godfrey stepped off the flying boat at La Guardia, New York. They were there to observe US port security alongside William Stephenson's[73] British Security Coordination[74] (BSC), who worked out of New York.

There was of course more to the trip than that.[75] The gentlemen from NID were overtly there to assist Stephenson in developing a security sector in America that would benefit both US and UK interests.[76]

Godfrey was keen to make William Donovan head of the new security force. Donovan was a senior partner in a law firm but during the Great War he had worked as a private intelligence gatherer for J P Morgan, so he was a known but albeit, unused officer. Fleming had tried to coax Donovan into Operation GOLDENEYE, but Godfrey had him personally earmarked for the US.

The duo had a strange trip to America inasmuch as they flew to Lisbon first and then onto New York via the Azores and Bermuda, something 'government officials' couldn't get away with – to this day – without some sound justification. They visited their intelligence gatherers in these places to see what news they could learn about American intelligence – and its potholes – prior to their visit.[77]

Once in New York they made their way to the St Regis Hotel, near Central Park, which had intelligence connections via its owner Vincent Astor; whose family worked closely with BSC.[78]

Fleming and Godfrey soon got to work, Fleming making contact with Stephenson, liking the man's serious compunction to work and never-ceasing energy. Stephenson told the duo about the nuances of his job. He mentioned the resistance he encountered from time to time from the Americans, especially J Edgar Hoover.

Hoover, as head of the FBI and the US State Department, didn't like having British spies in the US (that said, Hoover and Stephenson did sometimes collaborate in operations against espionage activities orchestrated by Nazi Germany in the US). They also made an agreement that the BSC would not hire Americans while in the US; which unfortunately they did![79]

At 12.31 hrs to 12.47 hrs on 6 June, Fleming and Godfrey had an audience with the FBI chief in Washington. Fleming later stated that Hoover 'received them graciously', and 'listened with close attention to our exposé of certain security problems, and expressed himself firmly but politely as uninterested in our mission.'

This wouldn't have come as such a great surprise to Stephenson, who was familiar with Hoover's arrogance, but Fleming and Godfrey were disappointed as they wanted to create a direct intelligence route to the FBI for NID. They had to content themselves with continuing to work through Stephenson.

Hoover didn't throw them out straight away. He made the trip a pleasant one for the two Englishmen: they were shown the FBI Laboratory and Record Department and taken to the basement shooting range, which would have thrilled Fleming immensely as he was interested in small arms.

That was the full extent of the meeting with Hoover but there was other work to be done. Godfrey was primarily in Washington to arrange a meeting with President Roosevelt.

He thought, initially, that he could do this through Hoover but alas not. He had to go back to Stephenson and see if he could arrange it.

Stephenson contacted Sir William Wiseman, his predecessor, and with the assistance of Arthur Hays Sulzberger, publisher of the *New York Times*, Godfrey was invited to a private dinner at the White House by Mrs Roosevelt. The president was sure to attend.

Godfrey met President Roosevelt at the dinner and was allowed to put his whole case across for a joint intelligence service that served both US and UK interests. The president listened and discussed every point with Godfrey, making the whole dinner-experience challenging to say the least for the DNI.

Godfrey stood his ground and responded well to the president's questions. He took his time and outlined his case magnificently, even suggesting Donovan as the deputy head of the new establishment.

On 18 June 1941 the president had a meeting with Donovan and made him Co-ordinator of Information (COI); his work: the collection of intelligence and planning of covert offensive operations. This work would then be passed on to the Office of Strategic Services (OSS).

All of this seems so easily achieved by Godfrey but it must be appreciated that Stephenson was an important part in the whole process. He lined up the important meeting with the president and did all the groundwork before Godfrey and Fleming ever went to the States.

So what did Fleming get up to while in the States? One interesting story, originally mentioned by John Pearson in his biography of Fleming, is important: the foiling of a Japanese cipher expert. This little incident was planned by Stephenson, who according to Pearson was 'a master of the technology of subversion'. Station M, the laboratory Pearson had set up in Canada under cover of the Canadian Broadcasting Corporation, claimed to be able to "reproduce faultlessly the imprint of any typewriter on earth". Fleming was enthralled.

The Japanese cipher expert worked on the staff of the Japanese Consul-General in New York – in the Rockefeller Centre on the floor below Stephenson's office!

Stephenson was aware that coded messages were being sent from his building to Tokyo and made it his mission to stop them. Fleming took part in this operation and later wildly exaggerated its detail as 'a shooting' in *Casino Royale* (when explaining one of the incidents that earned Bond his '00' licence in the first place).

Fleming was present when the Consul's office was searched. He was let in at approximately 03.00hrs to borrow the Japanese code books for an hour. It must have been exhilarating for Fleming to see duplicate keys prepared, safes cracked, items copied and put back exactly as they had been found. This was a seriously professional job.

Fleming didn't really enjoy America[80] but he did leave feeling that they – he and Godfrey – had achieved all that they had wanted. He also had a little keep-sake too. Donovan had presented him with a 38 Police Positive Colt revolver, with the inscription 'For Special Services'.

Fleming was mightily proud of his work and, years later, his memories of the trip became a little more 'rose-tinted', when he claimed that he was one of the creators of the Central Intelligence Agency (CIA). Although there are elements of truth in that, it is a vast over-simplification of what happened. Donovan's COI later developed into the OSS and from that came the CIA. Fleming was just one piece of the complex jigsaw that got the ball rolling. In fairness to Fleming, he did write a letter to Colonel Rex Applegate, a former US Army officer, in March 1957, stating that he had 'spent some time with [Donovan] in his house in Washington writing the original charter of the OSS'. So the generalisation was in a verbally hasty aside, rather than a boastful rant.

In his biography of Fleming, John Pearson secured the following quote from Ivar Bryce, who worked for Sir William Stephenson in Washington during Fleming's trip:

'Ian wrote out the charter for the American COI at General Donovan's request. He wrote it in longhand in a room in the British Embassy and it took just over two days. He wrote it as a sort of imaginary exercise, describing in detail all the arrangements necessary for financing, paying, organising, controlling and training a secret service in a country which had never had one before. It explained how this secret service fitted in with the other Departments of State. And it included a mass of practical detail on how much use could be made of diplomatic sources of intelligence, how agents could be run in the field, how records could be kept, and how liaison could be established with other governments.'

ADM 223/464, Enclosure 118 also states: 'Much depended on Colonel Donovan. At first, after DNI had left America and Commander Fleming had followed three weeks later, the principal contact with him was through Mr Stephenson, and Captain Hastings connection with him was "clandestine in order to avoid the charge of British influence and direction". Fleming had in fact prepared the majority of the memoranda in which Colonel Donovan put forward his case to the president and DNI had stayed as Donovan's guest in New York.'

Donovan obtained an initial grant of $10 million to set up the COI, but that didn't get him very far. A skeleton staff was put in place and because of the naivety of the Americans with regard to intelligence work, Stephenson had to do a great deal of spoon-feeding to get the COI on its feet. Donovan was good (especially with his experience with the UK SIS) but he was one man in a new intricate arena. He valued Fleming's advice and structure – hence the presentation of the gun – but he knew he had to move things on rapidly, especially after Pearl Harbour.

Hoover was also an obstacle. He didn't like contaminating his men. Also, as Thaddeus Holt explains in *The Deceivers – Allied Military Deception in the Second World War*: 'with all his faults, indeed to some extent because of them, Hoover had created one of the world's great police forces for conventional law enforcement and scientific criminal investigation. But at international intelligence and counter-intelligence work it was still a novice when the Second World War began.'

The OSS received its name and broad charter in June 1942 and that was when something close to Britain's MI6 was formed with some joined-up logic between the US and the UK.

Fleming had come home from America in late July 1941. Not only did he feel like he had achieved so much, he had some new ideas in his head as to how to push British intelligence work forwards. Donovan and Stephenson had also inspired his already active imagination during a short trip to Canada on the way home.

Stephenson had created a school for his potential recruits at Oshawa. A course had been designed in skills such as safe blowing, lock picking and housebreaking, as well as general endurance exercises. One such exercise had Fleming swimming underwater to attach a mine to a tank (a similar exercise as to that mentioned at the climax of *Live and Let Die*). In fact from this moment on, Fleming would enjoy underwater swimming.

Fleming took part in many of these activities and was exposed to certain specialist skills, such as the use of ciphers, the intricacies of audio/radio/listening devices and explosives. He even learnt some basic spying techniques.[81]

All of this certainly opened his eyes to the hidden world of government, where so much was possible covertly. We know that shortly before leaving NID, towards the end of the war, Fleming said that he intended to the write the 'spy story to end all spy stories', so the nucleus of James Bond was probably created by the time Fleming got back from Canada. However, before the fiction kicked in, Fleming would use that same influence to fuel something quite real and innovative. This would be called 30 Assault Unit, or as Fleming called them, his 'Red Indians'; a crack team of commandos who got their designation '30' from Fleming's secretary's door number in NID – the real Miss Moneypenny – as 30 AU veterans James 'Bill' Powell and Bill Thomas would call her.

> 'The harmony and good understanding between the Army and Navy employed on this occasion, will I trust be . . . proof of what may be effected by the hearty co-operation of the two services.'
>
> Lord Nelson

Chapter Ten

30 Assault Unit

'They were thinking what he was thinking, like himself they were
back several hours in time and several hundred miles in space in
that Admiralty Operations Room in London where Vice-Admiral
Rolland, ostensibly Assistant Director of Naval Operations but in
fact the long-serving head of MI6, the counter-espionage branch of
the British Secret Service, and his deputy, Colonel Wyatt-Turner,
had gravely and reluctantly briefed them on what they had as
gravely and reluctantly admitted to be a mission born from
the sheerest desperation.'

Where Eagles Dare
Alistair MacLean

There are hundreds of movies and novels that concern
themselves with covert commando operations during the
Second World War, but despite their all-action appeal, how
much of their disparate stories are based upon solid fact?
The short answer is: they have some semblance of fact in
them, especially as some of the writers – such as Alistair
MacLean – had seen action. MacLean's first novel, *HMS
Ulysses,* was solidly based upon the author's own wartime
experiences and fuelled a bestselling career that lasted
several decades.

In novels such as *Where Eagles Dare, The Guns of Navarone*
and *Force 10 From Navarone,* a crack team of commandos
face almost impossible odds. They also have some

semblance of fact through the early exploits of the SAS and naval intelligence commando unit: 30 Commando Unit (30 CU), later 30 Assault Unit (30 AU).[82]

30 CU were essentially a crack team of commandos formed by Ian Fleming. Fresh from Canada and filled with inspiration, Fleming drew up his plans for 30 CU, just as he had written the plan for the new American intelligence service while in the States.

It was in 1942 that Fleming created 30 CU: a unit of soldiers trained in lock picking, safe cracking, forms of armed combat and intelligence gathering. One could be brutal and suggest that if Fleming believed he provided the bones of the CIA then Donovan and Stephenson provided the blueprint for 30 CU; as they had introduced the tactics to Fleming in Canada.[83]

It has been said by many writers (and some historians) that Fleming planned all of 30 CUs operations with Patrick Dalzel-Job. This is not true. Dalzel-Job was not part of the unit before it became 30 AU.[84] Also – and quite importantly – Fleming wasn't the catalyst for everything 30 CU did, especially in the field, where his influence was virtually non-existent. In fact, he tried to pass the idea of 30 CU to another department in his original memo, something Godfrey quickly countered in his formal response (not wishing another department to take the credit).

30 CU didn't just come out of Fleming's experiences in Canada, there was a military influence too. In May 1941, the island of Crete was lost. Amongst the first Nazi officers in there was *Obersturmbandfuehrer* Otto Skorzeny. Navy Intelligence officers learnt that Skorzeny had a specific role in the capture of Crete: to gather as much British Secret material from British headquarters in Maleme and Heraklion as possible. He quickly got in and then quickly got out again. This rapid action impressed Fleming very much. Skorzeny was head of a group of Intelligence Commandos and Fleming instantly saw the benefit of

setting up a similar unit, using the skills he had acquired – seen – in Canada. So two disparate things came together to create 30 CU. Fleming would continue to gather intelligence about Skorzeny after the formation of the unit, which various parts of British intelligence was interested in.

Fleming undoubtedly had Skorzeny in mind while writing *Moonraker* (he would be mentioned by name in the book as somebody Sir Hugo Drax worked for) so the individual did continue to fascinate him well after the Second World War and at least into the 1950s.[85]

Let us now look at the growth of 30 CU after Fleming's original idea. After much conversation amongst the staff of NID, Fleming raised the proposal of 30 CU formally. During 1942 JIC accepted it in the form of a proposal put forward by DNI for the 'operation of an intelligence assault unit for participation in commando raids'. A special unit of the Special Service Brigade was formed and designated No 30 Commando. A small section of this unit operated with success in the landings in North Africa and later took part in clear up operations in Tunisia. Increased to a strength of approximately fifty, including all ranks and later reinforced by the temporary seconding of specialist officers and Admiralty Scientists, 30 Commando did good work in Sicily and Italy, capturing a substantial quantity of documents and equipment of operational value.

During this period a system was created of working in small self-contained field teams (a section) consisting of two officers and about six or eight other ranks carried in a 15 cwt lorry, left some two or three miles behind the front line the team then advanced upon its objectives either on foot or riding on the backs of AFVs. Good results were also obtained by small-scale raiding parties landing from the sea. During this period the efficiency of the unit suffered from inadequate intelligence briefing and the lack of a trained headquarters staff.[86]

The unit returned to the UK towards the end of 1943 in

order to reform for the invasion of NW Europe. By this time numbers were considerably strengthened, the Royal Marines (RM) wing being brought up to about 150 strong and additional specialists attached to the Royal Navy (RN) wing – the Army wing was released for other duties. A small headquarters staff was provided and adequate preparations made, by the production in NID, for a Black List of Admiralty intelligence requirements and objectives.[87] The RN and RM wings were administered and commanded independently from the Army wing at this time.

Under the designation 30 AU, the unit participated in the landings on D Day and in operations in France (see Chapter Eleven where more detail is supplied about the unit from this moment on). However this period did not prove very fruitful and the new system of attaching large bodies of 30 AU to regular battalions did not work and was something Fleming was bitterly against from the beginning. Indeed, it caused friction with the regular army and the Allies. Documentation in the National Archive suggests that the divided chain of command was to blame i.e. being 'unworkable in practice', but I suspect it was more to do with the conflict in operational duties. 30 AU had to go in ahead and do a specialist job of gathering intelligence before it was destroyed; they weren't fighting, liberating, of pushing the enemy backwards. In short, 30 AU were getting all the exciting jobs while the regulars were getting the dull ones: the regulars had to wait for 30 AU and 30 AU had to wait for the regulars.

Most of the documented missions of 30 AU were successful in attaining their objectives. This measure of success is considered to have derived from:

i) The calibre of certain individual officers and their equipment.

ii) The thorough basic training of all ranks, which resulted in a general understanding of the principles of the work undertaken.

iii) The efficiency of the unit's motor transport, small boats and other means of movement.[88]

iv) The fact that the unit consisted almost entirely of combatant personnel and consequently could operate with the forward troops.

v) Adequate headquarters staff.

vi) Efficient planning and briefing.

This latter point is clearly showcased with the unit's first real piece of business: in early 1942 Fleming saw the first real opportunity of using his crack team of commandos, albeit with precious little time to prepare. Navy intelligence had become involved in the first full-scale attack on the French coast, specifically the harbour installations at St Nazaire. Fleming discussed his ideas with Godfrey and the opportunity arose to form a small group of intelligence commandos as part of a large raid on Dieppe. Two naval lieutenants, backed by ten tough marines were assigned to smash their way into the Nazi headquarters and gather as much intelligence as possible. It was a crude, rushed idea, but it got the nod of approval. Fleming asked to accompany the unit but his wish was declined (yet again[89]). He was allowed to follow the unit's progress from a British ship, but this only added to his frustrations when the Canadian fighting forces were held up and the attack went pear-shaped: Fleming's unit wouldn't be activated, a failure due to poor planning.

Godfrey wouldn't allow his 'Naval Intelligence Assault Unit' to crumble after such a bad show. Once properly formed and pending the grant of its own establishment, the unit was placed temporarily under the command of Commander RED Ryder, VC, RN, a member of CCO's naval training staff. Major W.G. Cass, The Buffs, a regular officer with considerable experience of Army B Intelligence, was appointed second in command, while Fleming merely represented DNIs interests. This explains the cock-up of the unit becoming disparate around the time of D Day – Fleming wasn't in charge and the unit was moving away from his original idea.

In November 1942 a war establishment was granted to the unit under the cover name of the 'Special Engineering Unit of the Special Service Brigade'. An office for the planning staff was allotted and an independent headquarters at Amersham, where the troops were billeted in private houses.

The original organisation was as follows:

Commanding Officer: Cdr Ryder VC, RN
Second in Command: Major Cass, The Buffs

No 33 (RM) Troop:
Two captains RM
20 other ranks RM

No 34 (Army) Troop:
Two captains (later to increase to four)
12 other ranks

No 36 (RN or 'technical') Troop:
Lt Cdr RNVR
Lts RNVR
S/Lts RNVR

Of the officers involved in the organisation, those designated as long-term patrons were:

QTPM Riley RNVR
Lieut DMC Curtis RNVR
Sub-Lieut G McFee

Because I have been keen throughout this book to illustrate the text with the real personality of individuals who worked with Fleming, it is therefore interesting to learn a little about these exceptional officers, who became the pioneers in 30 AU:

Lieutenant Commander Riley was a graduate of Cambridge University. Between 1930 and 1937 he was engaged continuously on polar exploration, taking part in two expeditions to Greenland and one to the Antarctic. He joined the RNVR in 1939 but was transferred temporarily to a special battalion of the Scots Guards, which had been mobilized to operate in Finland. This campaign did not materialise, however, and Lieutenant Commander Riley returned to RNVR serving on the staff of Brigadier Gubbins in Norway where he was mentioned in Despatches. On his return he was appointed to Combined Operations as a Flotilla Officer and eventually served in Iceland as instructor in winter warfare. On his recovery from injuries received in this service, he was selected by Commander Ryder for 30 Commando.

Lieutenant Curtis graduated at Oxford and completed his studies on the continent. He became a solicitor in 1935, joined the RNVSR in 1936 and was called up to RNVR in Feb 1940. He served at first in Coastal Forces and took part in the raids of St Nazaire and Dieppe. For his part in the former he received the immediate award of the DSC. Subsequently he was engaged in special operations in home waters with DDOD(I) and joined 30 Commando on its formation. Lieutenant Curtis was fluent in French and German.

S/Lieutenant Mc Fee was an Incorporated Accountant and at the outbreak of war held a position in the Accounts Department of the City Treasurer of Dundee. He joined the

RNVR under the 'Y' scheme, and on receiving his commission volunteered for hazardous service.[90] As a consequence he was appointed to 30 Commando.

Some of the key men in 30 AU, included: Robert Harling (mines and minefields), Ralph Izzard (V1 and V2 expert) and Patrick Dalzel-Job (intelligence recovery) and later Charles Wheeler.[91]

The unit as a whole received the following programme of basic training:

i) Assault and street fighting course on the usual commando lines.

ii) The handling of small arms, mortars and hand grenades.

iii) Enemy mines and booby traps.

iv) The handling of explosives, demolitions and counter-demolitions.

v) The recognition of enemy uniforms, badges, weapons and vehicles.

In addition, the RN and Army Troops, together with a few of the Royal Marines, were instructed in:

i) Parachute jumping.

ii) The handling of small boats.

iii) The recognition of enemy documents.

iv) The searching of premises and recovery of material from salvage, safe breaking and lock picking.[92]

v) The searching of persons and the care of prisoners of war.

vi) The recognition of individuals from photographs and descriptions.

vii) Escaping drill, instruction for activities as prisoners of war and conduct under interrogation.

The RN and Army troops also took an intensive course in the photography of equipment and documents.[93]

The officers of the RN troop, who were regarded as specialists in the intelligence aspects of the unit's activities, were divided into groups to take courses in enemy sea mines, torpedoes, electronics, hydrophones and asdic gear, the internal layout of submarines, the organization of enemy Armed Forces and intelligence services, and also languages (primarily German and Italian). Certain officers also qualified as divers.

Fleming found that administration duties kept him from becoming directly involved in the real action of 30AU; a matter which Dalzel-Job probably didn't understand when he joined the unit (in a timely manner before D Day). Dalzel-Job looked upon Fleming with something approaching disdain.

However, Fleming didn't help himself by simplifying the whole structure for his peers to understand: 30 AU were created in London as NID 30. Their task was to go ahead of Allied troops, or at least lead an assault, in order to capture papers and equipment, essentially of naval interest, before such things could be destroyed by enemy troops, A, B and X troop in the field. NID 30 planned the strategies and then became 30 AU to execute the plans in the field.

Fleming could be dictatorial, perhaps why he was disliked so much by some of his peers and contemporaries.[94] He clucked around 30 AU like a mother hen with her chicks, upsetting many people along the way due to the special privileges he arranged for his unit. For example, unlike most units, 30 AU had direct access to the Admiralty, mainly to Fleming himself, but also to other officers (through Fleming) when the need arose. This was irregular but then again, because Fleming was not that well versed in the protocols of the Royal Navy, he did things to suit him and his unit, not anyone else; and felt quite justified in doing so. Let us look at the detail of his very first success with 30 Commando (as they were then); this clearly illustrates their odd way of doing things and how they rubbed up colleagues in the military but still got results.

On 8 November 1942, 30 Commando was aboard HMS *Sheffield* wearing American GI uniforms and British naval officer cap badges. They looked – to the military mind – like a bunch of mercenaries. Their mission statement was clear, even if how to implement it wasn't. 30AU were affectively a deep penetration unit and because of this, coherent, strategic plans had to be written in the field (as nobody could know how the enemy would react once a campaign had started). Logic had to be applied to the case in hand; otherwise huge risks would be taken for no reason.

30 Commando didn't stay aboard HMS *Sheffield* very long; as Fleming discovered. The landing from the ship had to be abandoned because of the heavy fire from the harbour guns. HMS *Broke*, a British destroyer, was seriously damaged and 30 Commando had to go ashore via HMS *Malcolm*. This had never been catered for in NID 30. But 30 Commando in the field adapted, overcame, and found themselves in Sidi Ferruch, west of Algiers. They commandeered a lorry, holding its driver at gun-point, and made their way cross-country until they found the Italian naval headquarters.

30 Commando took the headquarters by surprise and captured all the intelligence and sent it back to the

Admiralty via Gibraltar. This, their first operation, had been a resounding success and Fleming could bask in his own glory. His unit had proved themselves. Not only that, the intelligence they had arrested was of high quality: enemy cipher messages, orders and battle plans. The treasure was indeed bountiful.

It was because of this success that Fleming was assigned some Royal Marines to support the unit. He was flying high now, but just when he thought everything was rosy Godfrey was moved on to become Flag Officer, Royal Indian Navy. This was a major blow for Fleming because Godfrey was more than just a boss. He was a friend, confidant and a 'mover and shaker in high places'. They had really bonded, but now, quite naturally, Fleming would have his wings clipped until such a time as he could break-in the new boss (if indeed he could). He had to resign himself to being a personal assistant again and being a little less bolshie.

Godfrey was replaced by Commodore E G N Rushbrooke but Fleming had little to worry about as far as his reputation was concerned: 30 Commando had driven along the coast of North Africa to meet Monty's Eighth Army. Not only that they had captured a map of enemy minefields and defences at Sicily. Rushbrooke could sense that Fleming was on a roll with his commando unit; and let it run the gauntlet. If Fleming had bad luck with Operation RUTHLESS and some level of dissatisfaction with Operation GOLDENEYE (because it couldn't be put into practice and was deemed too elaborate) he had proved himself through his intelligence commandos.

But 30 Commando didn't take up all his time. He still had his day-to-day chores to see to and, something else: since August 1941 Fleming had taken a great interest in black and white propaganda (white was put out by BBC; black by other groups to confuse the enemy) through the newly formed Political Warfare Executive (PWE). Fleming, as a

German speaker, delivered speeches for BBC German Services: he would comment on leaky U-boats and how fool-hardy the Japanese were for bombing Pearl Harbor and getting America into the war. On the whole, Fleming's contributions were not earth-shattering. But in 1942, when the war in the Atlantic was at its most ferocious and all hands went to the pump, he assisted Sefton Delmer's black propaganda operation (conducted from PWE Woburn Abbey) to decoy Nazi U-boat crews from Allied convoys.

A new unit entitled 17Z was also set up, headed by Donald McLachlan.[95]

McLachlan would soon set up two bogus radio stations, Deutscher Kurzwellensender Atlantik and Soldatensender Calais, and do his best to ruin the U-boat crews' morale.

Rushbrooke could see that Fleming was on top of his job, with many fingers in a multitude of pies. He also had sight of a glowing report left by Godfrey dated 10 December 1942, the crux of it stating: '[Fleming] has conducted himself very greatly to my satisfaction. His zeal, ability, and judgement are altogether exceptional.' This was high praise indeed, so the transfer from Godfrey to Rushbrooke was not as major as some would believe; Rushbrooke would simply observe Fleming with a cool military eye and guide him when such military experience was needed.

'My accelerated promotion to Lieutenant Commander ... was promulgated a few days after I started work in Admiralty. Commander Fleming was obviously delighted, but I soon understood that the real reason for this was that it added to his own prestige to have a Lieutenant Commander in "his" unit.'

Arctic Snow to Dust of Normandy
Patrick Dalzel-Job

Chapter Eleven

Patrick Dalzel-Job joins in

'It was my good fortune that two splendid Royal Marines from
30 Commando were allocated to me; they stayed with me through
the rest of the war and afterwards, in good times and bad.'

Arctic Snow to Dust of Normandy
Patrick Dalzel-Job

In the last chapter I discussed the formation of 30 Commando
(later 30 AU) and some of the people associated with it.

I would like to move on now and discuss the unit's work
in Europe through Patrick Dalzel-Job. I do this for several
reasons: it is important to focus in on one unit within 30 AU
and explore the detail of its work[96] as well as showcase some
of the dangers the unit faced in theatre. This will also show
how removed Dalzel-Job was from Fleming and temper the
romanticism around Dalzel-Job, who has been ear-marked
as the real-life James Bond (a rumour he was indifferent to);
but at the same time showcase his remarkable contribution
to the unit.

In his autobiography, Patrick Dalzel-Job stated that 'he
discovered an outfit called "30 AU"'. He wasn't head-
hunted to join the team. For somebody who would become
such a key figure in the unit, it is slightly disappointing that
Dalzel-Job had to choose the unit as opposed to the other
way around. One would expect his peers to find him the
obvious choice; but he wasn't.

In a way Dalzel-Job was a little like Fleming. He didn't quite fit convention. His father died during the Great War and he sailed a small brigantine with his ageing mother along the Arctic coast of Norway, where he set up home until the outbreak of the Second World War. He then became an intelligence officer volunteering his services to the Royal Navy.

He was detached from his wartime post in as much as he could see his bizarre – eccentric – senior officers for the potential harmful bystanders they sometimes were. His view of Fleming was sober indifference and his own practical skills and qualities of leadership were second to none.

Perhaps the greatest illustration of Dalzel-Job's personality traits was his adoration for a blue-eyed Norwegian school girl called Bjorg Bangsund. Shortly before the war, Bjorg became a deckhand on the *Mary Fortune* (Dalzel-Job's brigantine) but she soon went away to safety after the outbreak of the war and Dalzel-Job volunteered his services to the British Armed Forces. It wasn't very soon after the end of the war that Dalzel-Job made his way back to Norway, found Bjorg, now in her late teens and married her, after three weeks of being reunited. This was so typically Bond: the man who wanted to jack in the fighting to lose his heart to the sweetest girl he'd ever met and live happily ever after.[97]

I have the distinct impression that Fleming had much more regard for Dalzel-Job than the officer had for the future novelist; because when one reads Dalzel-Job's autobiography, one clearly picks up the indifference to Whitehall and longing for true love – attributes Fleming gave Bond and indeed, embraced himself.[98] But Dalzel-Job was a physical man and applied his can-do attitude and intelligence in the field at any given opportunity. He was a natural intelligence commando even though he hadn't been exhaustively trained to be so. He had learnt practical seamanship by navigating his way across the channel; he was his own man:

self-assured, practical, reliable, intelligent, meticulous, passionate.

When one looks through the records at the crack team that became 30 AU, it is not surprising that with the correct structure, training and hands-on success, they had more money thrown at them to purchase the equipment they needed to do the job properly. On file at the National Archive there are sums of money being designated to department for quick payment, in different currencies for 30 AU equipment. There was no time wasting. If they needed something they got it.[99] Their personal weaponry was quite impressive: Fairbairn-Sykes Commando Knife,[100] Colt M1911A1 pistol, SMLE No1 MK111, Lee Enfield No4 rifle, Thompson M1928A1, Sten M1 SMG, Bren MG and Mills grenades.

Dunstan Curtis was the senior naval officer when Dalzel-Job joined. Curtis had been promoted in post and had proved himself to be an excellent officer. Dalzel-Job rated Curtis highly, bowing down to his experience and ability. Although a novice to the type of work expected of him in 30 AU, Dalzel-Job would soon be dragged up-to-speed by vigorous training and intense planning within the Admiralty. As previously mentioned, 30 AU were NID 30 in office, and much went into their planning of operations.

One of the first things Dalzel-Job worked on was D-Day. Along with Curtis and Riley he plotted where the enemy's secret documents would be stored, based upon the intelligence that was at hand – sparse though it was. They worked in an isolated office called the 'Citadel'.[101]

The Citadel was quiet, cut off, the hub of secrecy. A perfect place to conceive and plot operations. The atmosphere was always intense and formal. Not just because they were writing orders based upon their interpretation of the intelligence, but because it was them who would have to implement those orders in the field. They were literarily taking their own lives in their hands, planning deep-penetration exercises into enemy territory.

Dalzel-Job described this way of working as 'a good arrangement. The theory was that the Naval officer would direct strategically and then be escorted to the designated "Target" by a troop from the Royal Marine Commando; as with such theories of combined command, it did not work that way and in practice whoever was most senior took tactical as well as strategic command, regardless of service.

Fleming's touch is very clear in the above description of the working process of NID 30/30 AU: completely unorthodox for its time and built solely for the user. Of course Fleming would oversee his 'Red Indian's' work; although Commander Curtis later stating that Fleming would get 'terribly excited, as though it was him that was going on the mission instead of just us'. They were living Fleming's dream; just as the fictional James Bond would later do.

Before D Day 30 AU were all issued with special passes, which 'by command of General Eisenhower' gave authorization for them to be self-contained. Their passes stated: 'the bearer of this card will not be interfered with in the performance of his duty by the military police or by other military organisation'. 30 AU knew virtually everything about the plans for D Day in advance except the actual date and precise landing place. They were indeed very privileged, and this naturally caused animosity from the other units.[102] Likewise for Fleming too, who became known as 'The Chocolate Soldier', a title he hated but that was mild criticism compared to what some people were saying about him!

It was on 4 June 1944 that 30 AU were moved to 'the Cage', a security camp near Chichester. The place was quite ominous as it was surrounded by barbed wire and completely cut-off from outside life. Again – not unlike the Citadel, 30 AU was left to its own devises in order to make good all their preparations for the big day. And once that was done, they waited.

They needed good weather to start the operation. It didn't come quickly. So they continued to wait. All the men could do was keep fit; Dalzel-Job running five miles a day, but found it unusually tiring. Although, he mentioned in his autobiography that the time he spent in 'the Cage' was almost like a holiday for him. There had been little let up in his war, so he enjoyed the respite and, also, the companionship. Dalzel-Job's bodyguard was Bill Wright, 'a bright young lad . . . [who] I owe my life several times over'. The other man he remained close to from 'the Cage' until after the war was his driver 'Lofty' Frazer, a tall red-haired Glaswegian, who taught Dalzel-Job how to drive.

All too soon, the lieutenant-colonel Royal Marines was addressing the unit prior to embarkation. 30 AU was split into two groups. The first went ashore with the first British troops on D Day, without loss, but the rest – including Dalzel-Job – worked with the Americans and Canadians initially, and landed near Varreville on Utah Beach on 10 June (D + 4).[103]

Dalzel-Job mentioned in his autobiography that there was 'some trouble getting away from the beach; but the lieutenant-colonel set out to overtake the columns of American troops that were moving towards the front line'. The Colonel failed to achieve this and the unit momentarily had to play second fiddle to the Americans.

It wasn't exactly plain sailing though. The back-packs weren't the heaviest Dalzel-Job had ever carried – his time doing recognisance in the field at Norway was more painfully irksome in that respect – but the Normandy roads were hot and sticky and made for an uncomfortable time. Even the elite felt weary.

30 AU had split their packs evenly. Dalzel-Job carried plastic explosive sticks (for blowing up safes), while Marine Wright carried the detonators. This dovetailing of different personnel knitted 30 AU together more tightly (although Wright was Dalzel-Job's bodyguard the pair also worked as

a cracking duo of equal importance). Although 30 AU could be a disparate group, they were a professional team of commandos who acted as one in the field. The commandos wore their green berets with pride, which upset General Patton for one.[104]

One can appreciate Fleming's love for 30 AU. He had battled to see his good idea be put into practice and once it had he was keen to make it successful. When he accomplished that, he wanted them to build on that success. As we have seen, the unit started off well but the current operation was a big showcase, so much was at stake.

They jogged along the road in single file. The enemy was still some way ahead but they wouldn't engage with them that day. An hour after dark, they found the perfect camp for the night. A field surrounded by hedges. They started to settle down but as soon as they did the field was transformed into daylight with flashes and explosions. After 30 seconds a third of the unit had been wounded or killed. They had been attacked by butterfly bombs, which were released in the air from a large canister, whereupon they would spread out and explode all over the field in a shower of splinters.

Dalzel-Job explained that Bill Wright had been hit in the back and was rolling around in agony. Another chap also by the name of Wright had a tiny shard of the bomb pierce his neck, leaving only the tiniest of wounds, without blood. He was dead before he hit the floor.

Knowing that he could do nothing for the dead man, Dalzel-Job dropped to his knees to assist Bill Wight. He pulled up the man's battle dress and breathed a silent sigh of relief. A jagged piece of steel had hit the centrepiece of Wright's Army braces leaving a hell of a bruise but no serious damage. He quickly told Wright whose mood improved greatly with the knowledge. 'That bomb had my name but not my number on it,' Wright declared.[105]

Dalzel-Job then concerned himself with the other wounded men scattered around the field, using his torch he

could see that most of them had some pretty bad wounds –
two at least fatal – but despite these terrible injuries, the men
remained upbeat. Dalzel-Job found this reaction 'humbling'
and bandaged the men the best way he could.

Dalzel-Job would later note that the unit had made one
fundamental mistake: they hadn't cut a slit-trench to bed
down in[106]. If they had done so, most of the injuries wouldn't
have happened. Dalzel-Job would ensure that this mistake
would never happen again.

Even after the mission in Europe 30 AU were as unloved
as ever, General George Patton referred to them as 'Limy
gangsters' at one stage, although they did carry out some
deeply heroic activities, in some cases instigated by
American intelligence.

In June 1944 the unit was told that there appeared to be
a gap in enemy lines through which 30 AU could reach a
V1 site (this was still four months before British
Intelligence learned of a factory in Luxumberg that was
making the first elements of the V2 rocket). The V1 would
be used during the first ever terrorist attacks on the
civilian population of Great Britain. Dalzel-Job would not
have known at that precise time what fear the Vengence
machines of Hitler would cause, but he was keen to do
what he could to raid one of the sites if the opportunity
was there. Approval for a Royal Marine patrol, led by
Dalzel-Job, was given. As always, Bill Wright was chosen
as right-hand man, while a sergeant called Paul McGrath
led the unit – who Dalzel-Job remembered as a 'good,
steady man'.

The patrol penetrated enemy lines and like a creepy
Narnia, they found themselves in a rural but empty land.
They travelled quickly but cautiously through fields, either
on their belly's or bent double. One trick they employed was
always getting the last man to beckon to an imaginary next
man to follow him; this tactic had been proved to save the
lives of many commandos beforehand, as the enemy would

instinctively hesitate before firing (believing that the unit was bigger than it was).

Using a compass and the bearing of a church spire, the patrol soon found the V1 site. There was a concrete block house and runway, and much equipment just left hanging round. No one seemed very impressed by the scene except the experts who were led there later on that day – ironically the day the first V1s fell on London.

Aside from the V1 site, most of Dalzel-Job's time in Normandy was boring. His main job was making a slow advance on Cherbourg. Once there, they could undertake more duties for which they were specifically trained: raiding German underground headquarters and storage depots.

Dalzel-Job, like most talented officers, hated conformity. He excelled when he was allowed to think on his feet and travel ahead of the pack. Strangely, it was around this time, that Fleming began to get irritated that 30 AU were being treated like ordinary infantry soldiers and given rudimentary tasks to do but in truth, aside from the odd suicide mission (sic) there was little else for them to do at that time.

It must be stressed that 30 AU had a very tight brief. If something was not part of that brief, it wasn't done. In that respect, perhaps 30 AU/Fleming, were a little aloof: they wouldn't listen to any instructions that weren't in their little black books.

On 9 July 1944 Dalzel-Job entered Caen by jeep with Wright and driver 'Lofty' Fraser. There was so much rubble piled high across the road, it was totally impassable. The officer had to leave Fraser in charge of the vehicle and proceed on foot with Wright.

There was still much street fighting and one man they encountered was Sergeant Bramah, a British glider pilot, who had been injured when his glider crashed. He had evaded the enemy and then joined the French Resistance where he quickly became somewhat of a legend. Bramah became a useful assistant to Dalzel-Job and, uncharacteristically for a British officer, liaised with the enthusiastic French Resistance in his day-to-day work; they would come out of cellars and ruined buildings to guide Dalzel-Job and Wright onwards to the targets designated for their specialist duties. Dalzel-Job would later comment that the Americans used to completely ignore the French Resistance while the British were almost as bad. He considered this a great shame, as their local knowledge and keenness would have proved to be as important to the Allies as it was to Dalzel-Job.

Once the work had been completed the duo returned to their jeep. There were shell holes all around it but Fraser seemed more interested in trying to get his portable stove to work than worry about a life threatening mortar attack!

It was at this stage that Dalzel-Job was given a number two in the form of Charles Wheeler, a Royal Marine and excellent linguist. They took to each other straight away. Together they ransacked a half-submerged German patrol boat while the enemy took pot-shots at them; Wheeler had found an old raft and using two planks of wood as paddles the duo rode out to the ship. Once they had recovered some interesting booty, they loaded a more sea-worthy raft from the ship and got back to load up their jeep and drive away at pace.

Dalzel-Job considered this great fun and was impressed with Wheeler's daring-do. Dalzel-Job had a kindred spirit in Wheeler. Wheeler would become his right-hand man, pushing Marine Wright a little to the left (at the very least, Wright seems to have less of a mention in 30 AU files, such as HW 8/104, which details the history of the unit and Dalzel-Job's autobiography from here-on).

I'm sure Wheeler shared Dalzel-Job's frustration at having to advance with the Americans – an exercise that continued to go painfully slow but something 30 AU had to persevere with.

There were different types of soldier during the Second World War: those who joined up beforehand as career soldiers, those who were conscripted; and those who found their way there through other routes (mainly different areas of expertise). The latter category is where Dalzel-Job comes in. Although I single him out in this book because of the Fleming/Bond connection, he is also the catalyst for 30 AU in the field. His mindset to play war games a different way, to learn from experience and enjoy the thrill of extreme front-line activity is indicative of the whole ethos of 30 AU. It wasn't the place for regular soldiers. I am not diminishing regular soldiers, conscripted or otherwise, what I am doing is isolating a group of men who lusted after the thrill of the chase – not battle. 30 AU, as you have clearly seen by this time, were not a guerrilla force. Yes, they'd smash their way into HQs, but the taking of lives, pushing the enemy backwards, was not their priority – their priority was intelligence, the whole framework of what future operations were built upon. They were the James Bond characters who would locate the secret base – the German HQ – attack it, arrest the information from it and stop the world being blown up by a madman. It is very clear to me, at least, that Fleming had constructed the idea of his 'spy story to end all spy stories' by developing his creativity through the little operations he concocted for himself in NID, and those he worked on for 30 AU in the field.

As a conclusion to this chapter and for quick reference, I list the members of 30 AU detailed in this, previous chapter (along with a few extra names from Dalzel-Job's autobiography). If anyone wishes for a more detailed and structured list, including the different troops, I refer the reader to my sister work – *Ian Fleming's Red Indians – The History of 30 Assault Unit* (Pen & Sword, 2008), or the other associated works mentioned at the back of this book:

30 Assault Unit
Formed by: Commander Ian Fleming
Cmdr: Dunstan Curtis
Cmdr: 'Red' Ryder
Cmdr: Patrick Dalzel-Job
Lt Cmdr: Quintin Riley
Lt Cmdr: Jim 'Sancho' Glanville
Capt: 'Red' Huntingdon Whiteley
Major: W G Cass
RM Sgt: Paul McGrath
S/Lt: G McFee
RM Cpl: Wright (killed)
Staff Sgt: Bramah (attached to unit while working with French Resistance)
RM Capt: Charles Wheeler
Lt: Tony Hugill
Lt: Alec Van Cleef (died in service)
Bill Wright
James Powell
J 'Lofty' Fraser
Miles Cook
Johnny Rose
Bob Genfell
Ralph Izzard

Dazel-Job had the highest regard for his colleagues in 30 AU:

> 'Men trained and experienced . . . as well as being trained to fight, ought to be regarded as skilled tradesmen, and paid as such. It is no excuse for not so treating them that there is no demand for their special skills outside the armed services.'
>
> *Arctic Snow to Dust of Normandy*
> Patrick Dalzel-Job

Chapter Twelve

A Best Kept Secret

'We didn't know what other sections within 30 AU did and for you
to research it now makes a devil of a job.'

James 'Bill' Powell, Veteran 30 AU,
in conversation with the author

It is not the remit of this book to give an in-depth study of
30 AU but to simply explain what they did and how Ian
Fleming interacted with them once in the field.

Dalzel-Job stated that Fleming never took part in 30 AU
operations and only appeared once (at Carentan when they
rested and revised plans) but 'he didn't stay long'.

Looking over the detail of 30 AU in the field, it is clear to
see a lot of coincidences with the JPS deception strategies
constructed by Bevan and Wheatley, such as TORCH,
HUSKY and OVERLORD; they took part in them all.[107]
Papers in the National Archive confirm that the work of 30
AU,[108] from its inception, was very important to the JPS and
their work – GOLDENEYE was also discussed – was
brought up regularly during their meetings.

Also, as we have seen in the last chapter, 30 AU captured
a V1 site in enemy territory. This incident cannot be underestimated, because the findings were of major importance
to the newly formed Crossbow Committee (which included
Churchill and Alanbrooke) and their plans for thwarting
the V1s.[109] It is known that 30 AU progressed this work and

went on to provide intelligence for Operation BIG BEN – the anti-V2 Spitfire Missions. BIG BEN was the codename for V2 rocket and specially made clipped-winged Spitfire Mark XVIs headed dive-bombing missions on these sites.[110]

Flight Lieutenant Raymond Baxter[111] was one of the men who flew throughout this campaign (1944-45) and was unaware where most of the intelligence came from.

Shortly before he died, Baxter met Eileen Younghusband who worked in the Filter Room during the Second World War. She told him that any time a V2 was spotted both her and her colleagues had to stand on a chair and shout 'Big Ben'.[112] Baxter was amazed by this knowledge; but was also baffled by Alanbrooke's declaration that the V2s were eventually thwarted by the British Army when they stormed the Dutch rocket sites at the end of the war. 'Typical bloody soldier,' Baxter declared to me and, to a degree, he was right.[113] The Royal Air Force, chiefly 602 and 603 Squadrons, did so much to keep the manufacture and firing of the V2 rockets down. They had some fantastic results despite poor weather conditions; but it was the additional intelligence that came from the ground, quite early on, that paved the way for the great RAF mission; intelligence gathered by patrols from 30 AU? It is likely and that was an important part of what Alanbrooke was alluding to.

Another important point concerns Fleming's obsession for checking aerial photographs. For operations such as BIG BEN they were incredibly important and this illustrates how ground work correlated with air work countered enemy activity successfully.

All of these supposed disparate operations come together like a huge jigsaw: ground troops, such as 30 AU, were split into small patrols and went off into occupied territories to spy and collect data – not just physical data but perceptions too.[114] This would then be fed back to Fleming who would have a vision of the bigger picture and disseminate that information to other areas and departments, maybe the JPS, but certainly the Crossbow Committee, SOE etc. It made sense to ensure that the units involved knew as little about the intelligence gathering as possible, just in case they were captured by the Nazis. Remember, Fleming wasn't allowed to go on any operation – at the order of Godfrey – because he knew far too many secrets and worked on too many covert operations. However, the soldiers in the field were dispensable; and the less they knew regarding the bigger picture the better (this was a common frustration in intelligence work).

So when Alanbrooke mentioned the British Army putting a stop to V2s he refers to the fact that they supplied incredibly important ground intelligence and eventually arrested the rocket sites in Holland. What he doesn't acknowledge is the work the RAF did in between, which directly saved civilian lives in London and the Home Counties.[115] My point is quite a simple one: without the true professionals of both 30 AU and 602/603 Squadrons, brought together by NID, the Filter Room and the Crossbow Committee, none of the counter V rocket campaigns could have happened. No one was any more important than any one else, each had their significant role to play. And it is very important to realise that fact when assessing the validity of Top Secret units like 30 AU and likewise Top Secret campaigns like Operation BIG BEN.[116] Most of the people involved knew their role very well, but were oblivious – to their dying day – of what others did alongside them.

Something which we have seen clearly throughout this book is tension; tensions between desk officers in government departments right the way up to the specialist units fighting in the field. One could blame the stresses of war but these frustrations are also prevalent in times of peace and, at the lowest level, are nothing more than friendly banter. It simply escalates in times of crisis.

This illustrates another important point: lack of awareness. It is no secret that the hierarchy was blissfully unaware of a lot of Nazi plans, let alone how to counter them. This floundering would cause heated debates in Whitehall. In his memoirs Dennis Wheatley[117]mentioned the outlandish ideas of some people, including himself. But for all that, the good ideas were separated from the bad and the superior intelligence was separated from the poor and put out to the right people who could make it all work. I am labouring the point here but it must be appreciated that military histories only show one heroic moment, rarely do they show the wider picture, bringing in Whitehall and other areas of the Armed Forces who helped pull off so many strains of a major operation (especially the dull early work).

> 'The German V1 and V2... were never aimed at armies on land, ships at sea, nor indeed aircraft or airfields. Their purpose was to destroy, unhindered, the fighting spirit and capability of the British people.'
>
> Raymond Baxter, from his Introduction to
> *Operation Big Ben – the anti-V2 Spitfire Missions,*
> *1944–45*

Chapter Thirteen

Towards The End of Duty

'A blunt instrument wielded by a Government department. Hard, ruthless, sardonic, fatalistic. He likes gambling, golf, fast motor cars. All his movements are relaxed and economical'.

Ian Fleming describing James Bond,
in conversation with Jack Fishman
For Bond Lovers Only.

30 AU had grown from the intelligence gathering unit it had started out as and became the 'assault' squad its title demanded. Fleming was of course aware that if 30 AU became an out-and-out commando unit he would lose them completely. An exercise along the French coast with unit members disguised as fishermen was an important naval task and Fleming made it so. The photographs of the coast-line and important establishments (radar stations, harbours and factories), gave him quality intelligence for specific raids and other convert landings.[118]

To highlight specific naval tasks, Fleming gave Dunstan Curtis a detailed list of desirable pieces of equipment for 30 AU to acquire during their raids. Again, this was to separate their work from other commando units. If they could recover certain items and get them sent back to the Admiralty it would help with the important intelligence feed and counter enemy activity.

30 AU became a tenacious bunch, so much so, Fleming gave them the nick-name 30 'Indecent Assault' Unit.

On 15 August 1943, Fleming received a message from Curtis. He explained that important radar equipment had been captured by the unit at Douvres-la-Delivrande and was ready for transport back to Britain.

Fleming organised a high speed launch across the channel the following night to pick up the equipment and bring it home. Unfortunately the launch returned from Cherbourg without its bounty: 30 AU had forgotten all about it.

Fleming was outraged by this slapdash attitude. Suddenly it appeared that certain officers were getting a little too big for their boots. Fleming channelled his distaste through a message:

> *'Great trouble was taken to lay this craft on as you desired and it is indeed disappointing that the unit should have failed . . . in its side of the arrangements . . . to put it mildly, DDOD (I) is fed to the back teeth . . . I urge you not to continue questioning the decisions of DNI . . . under whose orders you operate. The position in Britanny and also in regard to Paris is perfectly clear here and we are fully informed on the progress of the campaign. Why you should imagine that this is not so, which is the only possible excuse for your attitude, I cannot understand.*[119] *The duties of the unit and its immediate role are also planned on the basis of more information than you can ever posses in the field.*
>
> *'One thing is certain and that is that unless the unit obeys its orders without question during the future stages of the campaign it will be impossible for me or Captain Lewes to prevent higher authority intervening drastically.'*

30 AU had been left to their own devices too long. They had formed opinions, made assumptions and plotted their own plans to an extent where they continued to think for themselves when orders arrived. They felt little was more

important than their work at the coal face; Whitehall had got things wrong and the Admiralty was just hot air and red tape. Then Fleming's note arrived and put them firmly in their place. The message was clear: NID held more intelligence than they could ever imagine, this was a school teacher talking down to pupil.

It was shortly after this episode that Fleming and Rushbrooke met with the men at Carteret, but the amount of time 30 AU had spent in theatre made them indifferent to Fleming's comments and pretentions. They just wanted to get on with their job.

And they did so, capturing a cellar of torpedoes at a mushroom farm near Houeilles, also being the first to capture a one-man submarine and turning it over to C-in-C of the Allied Expeditionary Force (Admiral Sir Bertram Ramsay). There biggest scoops came weeks before the end of the war with the ransacking of the Walterwercke (submarine works in Hamburg) and the torpedo experimental station in Eckernforder. These were profitable exercises, as they managed to gain great intelligence before the advancing Russians took choice pickings.

With the end in sight, Fleming then managed to see a little bit of the action. He knew that there was a castle called Tambach in the forests of Wurttemberg where much enemy documentation was being stored by an elderly admiral. Fleming and 30 AUs expert on enemy documentation (Trevor Glanville) decided to make the drive to Tambach and meet with the admiral. When they got there they found the General had made a mountain of documentation on the dried out bed of the lake, with the intention of burning it before the Russians could get their grubby hands on it (the pile of documents made up the whole of the German Navy archive going back to 1870).

Fleming befriended the old admiral and provided him with an alternative solution to burning his prized archive: letting the British have it instead. Fleming then organised a fishery protection vessel to bring the whole thing back to London where the admiral was given a job of assisting Fleming in editing the whole archive for posterity. This indeed was a great scoop for the budding writer and, probably gave the ancient mariner a lot of satisfaction too.

With the war practically over and the German Navy Archive in his possession, Fleming dashed off his last signal to 30 AU, which summed up his bravado at the time: 'find immediately the twelve top German naval commanders and make each one write ten thousand words on why Germany lost the war at sea.'

30 AU must have thought that their once glorious leader was taking the piss somewhat but frankly Fleming was past caring!

Fleming then went back to America, and on to Jamaica – where he fell in love with the place. He soon returned home where he found himself off to Colombo, Ceylon and Australia to talk about Navy intelligence in the Far East. At the beginning of March 1945 he was back in Jamaica, all roads seeming to culminate there. He stayed at Montego Bay with William Stephenson. The weather was beautiful and Fleming confided his plans for his own house in Jamaica to Lady Stephenson. The house was destined to be called Goldeneye.

Fleming was officially released from His Majesty's Service on 10 November 1945, with fifty-six days resettlement leave. Although he was back on civvy street again he wouldn't be able to forget the past five years and the work he – and his Red Indians – had done. It would colour his conversations – or small titbits would at least – and find its way into his novels as fictional set pieces. Of course there were elements he couldn't talk about but, as we see with *Moonraker*, the arrest of Nazi scientists by 30 AU and information from various V1 and V2 rocket installation whetted his appetite enough to inspire a story (even though he had to research the scientific part of it).

With Fleming's war over he became a newspaper man and slowly the articles turned into novels. Within ten years of the end of the Second World War 007, James Bond, would be born.

It is clear that Fleming used his wartime experiences in certain Bond novels, but he didn't over-do it, probably because of the Official Secrets Act and the D Notice slapped on the antics of 30 AU. Many Bond characters are deeply immersed in wartime characters. For example Fleming needed a quality armourer. This became Geoffrey Boothroyd, who gave him the knowledge of firearms and ostensibly made Bond look more professional; Fleming didn't possess the armourer's skills himself – he was an enthusiast when it came to in-theatre tactics.

Perhaps the best example of Boothroyd's influence on the Bond novels is in Chapter Two of *Dr No*, entitled 'Choice of Weapons'. In this piece, Bond gets to grips with his renowned Walther PPK 7.65 mm for the first time: '"It's a good gun, sir," Bond admitted. "Bit more bulky than the Beretta. How does the armourer suggest I carry it?"'

Because *Dr No* was the first James Bond movie, many people believe that Bond always carried the PPK. That isn't true. *Dr No* was the sixth book in the series: Boothroyd wrote and told Fleming that Bond was carrying the wrong gun after reading the early books (see Fleming's article 'The Guns of James Bond' for full details).

So despite his wartime experiences there were gaps in Fleming's knowledge but that is no harsh criticism of the man; civil servants in the Ministry of Defence today have a deep enthusiasm for 'kit' but because they are not trained to use it (in a military way) and can not work with it every day (mainly for Section Five clearance reasons) they remain enthusiasts.

Although Fleming died in the mid-1960s, one cannot knock his passion and drive for his work in NID or, indeed, his imaginative work creating the world of James Bond. He has left behind him a wonderful collection of fact and fiction, which we prize so highly today.

Like Dennis Wheatley – and to a lesser extent his own brother, Peter – Ian Fleming has carved his name deep into the history books of the twentieth century.

During the war the SOE was formed to take pressure off the Secret Service (and NID); but it was people like Fleming – and even Dennis Wheatley – that muddied the waters and put the onus back on their own departments. War, like a good football match, is won by creativity, often misunderstood as spontaneity.

> '. . . they formed SOE to try to straighten things out, and SOE found themselves up against the Secret Service and Naval Intelligence, OSS, MEW, G2 and all the others.'
>
> *The Diamond Smugglers*
> Ian Fleming

Chapter Fourteen

Diamonds Are Forever

'Today there are still dotted round the world powerful criminals living beneath a cloak of sunny respectability in an affluence which still comes from diamonds smuggled out of Africa.'

From 'John Blaize's Introduction to
The Diamond Smugglers

Once you are immersed in the covert world of intelligence it is difficult to get out. In fairness, many do not wish to. The high-brow networking and need to 'keep in touch' with the unseen world is strong. Many thriller writers are good examples of this from Dennis Wheatley to Frederick Forsyth.

We know that Fleming wished to write spy stories after NID and it took him the best part of ten years to do so. His first five Bond novels (up to *Dr No*) all have their NID influences. But then again, most writers' early works *are* influenced by their working lives.

Aside from the novels, Ian Fleming was always tempted back to the unseen parts of human nature. His capacity for ideas and lateral thought impressed the Kennedys' enough for him to be allowed to pursue those ideas through his own intelligence services. For example we can examine another intelligence trail through Fleming's first non-fiction *The Diamond Smugglers* (Jonathan Cape, 1957).

Released after his fifth novel *From Russia with Love*, *The Diamond Smugglers* examined the illegal trade of gems around the world in, what was essentially, the true-life counterpart to Fleming's fourth Bond novel *Diamonds Are Forever*.

In the introduction to the book, Blaize mentions that Fleming was a 'former naval intelligence officer', and was happy to play covert games in order to learn more about the multi-million pound illegal trade of gems that made the corrupt richer. So clear evidence here that Fleming still loved the cloak-and-dagger world of secret intelligence. He was happy to jump on a plane and fly to Tangiers to meet his contact for an assignation and the whole book includes such cloak-and-dagger characters as 'Frau X' and 'Mrs Y'; but is still highly readable despite the passing years (a pure blue-white polished diamond has increased in value some-what from £230!).

The photo section of the book has black and white images of 'big holes' cut deep in the ground (the Premier Mine of Pretoria) and huge corporate complexes, the multi-million pound plants that process the gems. Thus it is not such a leap of faith to see where the extravagant hideaways and larger-than-life characters of the Bond novels came from and it's not just the influence of *The Diamond Smugglers* that suggests this. Many of the characters Fleming met or analysed at NID and swapped stories about in the years following the Second World War (such as 'the enigmatic' Dr Lobo of Macao from another Fleming non-fiction *Thrilling Cities*, Jonathan Cape, 1963, who became the inspiration for the character of Dr No[120]) became characters in his books. The Nazis certainly played their part in *Moonraker* so very well, with real-life counterparts mentioned along the way (Otto Skorzeny).

When I spoke to James 'Bill' Powell during the research of this book, he told me that all the officers of 30 AU got decorated after the war but Fleming didn't. The reason being because he didn't see active service. But 30 AU was Fleming's idea. Both Powell and former 30 AU colleague Bill Thomas said that they had never met Fleming, because they were not officers, but they knew he was 'detested' in some quarters for the crack unit of commandos he created. But the elite usually are despised, because they make the people who – for whatever reason – don't make an effort, look pedestrian or stupid. In that respect perhaps Fleming was too intelligent for his own good, perhaps if he played by the Queensbury Rules he may have upset less people and obtained some recognition for his work. This book bares testament to his determination to do the right thing without compromise or self-glorification.

'Spies are trained to keep their mouths shut and they don't often lose the habit. That's why true spy stories are extremely rare, and . . . [I] have never seen one in print that rang completely true. Even in fiction there is very little good spy literature . . . perhaps only Somerset Maugham and Graham Greene and Eric Ambler have caught the squalor and greyness of the Secret Service.'

The Diamond Smugglers

Chapter Fifteen

Casino Royale –
Fleming's Dream of Secret Service

'James Bond was conceived and grew very slowly
in what used to be called Room 39 of the old Admiralty.'

Donald McLachlan

I believe it is important to discuss 'fact from fiction' when it comes to Ian Fleming. There are so many 007 lovers out there it is important to at least showcase, where the fact and fiction intertwined in Fleming's imagination to create James Bond.

The juxtaposition of Fleming, Bond and real-life Naval intelligence is not the main subject matter of a book; but it is of major interest and, there is no better example of the 'fact from fiction' debate than in the novel Casino Royale. Written at Goldeneye, Jamaica, from January to March 1952, the book's fabled ease in being written can be explained by its firm base in reality.

First, James Bond is a commander, Royal Navy, who has a love of Jamaica. So the character is not dissimilar to Fleming himself, with his house in Jamaica and wartime commission – albeit RNVR – of commander. This gives us some perspective to the 'juxtaposition' I mentioned: Bond was a 'paid up' member of the armed forces, while Fleming with a volunteer reserve. Couple this with the fact that Fleming's time at Sandhurst was painfully short-lived (as, ostensibly was his time as a subaltern in the Black Watch reserves). Here we have an underachiever as far as the armed forces is concerned. That underachiever's longing to play secret agent turned into the character – the fantasy – that is James Bond.

For further evidence, let us take a look at Fleming's time in Naval intelligence. He was an outsider. He hadn't seen action. He hadn't been taught the ways of the Royal Navy – the correct doctrine. He lacked a certain awareness that was both beneficial and detrimental to him (he could get away with saying and doing certain things because he hadn't been trained otherwise).

Fleming was a thinker, a planner, a brainstormer, privy to all intelligence and therefore never allowed to turn plans into actions. Ian Fleming was the epitome of the analogy 'a writer not a fighter'.

Sometimes his plans/would-be operations were scuppered, put off, or deemed unnecessary, due to time, relevance and money, so he threw into *Casino Royale* a huge – limitless – budget for the Secret Service and a no-nonsense style that was much applauded. When Bond gambles away a lot of money quite early on in the book, those 'in the know' applaud the fantasy. Bond is safe. He doesn't pose a threat to real-life espionage. But *Casino Royale* also has a 'firm base in reality'.

During their first night in Lisbon (1941), Admiral Godfrey and Commander Fleming dined at the luxury Aviz Hotel. The second night, they dined at the Estoril and went to play in its casino afterwards. It was here that the germ of an idea for *Casino Royale* was born. There was a group of Portuguese at the gambling table and Fleming mused to Godfrey that they were really Nazi agents and wouldn't it be fun to dent the Nazi fortune by cleaning them out? The reality was Fleming got cleaned out and he and Godfrey left for the United States of America the following day (to discuss a joint UK/USA intelligence agency).

So the germ of an idea for the first James Bond novel came from a Walter Mitty moment of Fleming's while working for Naval intelligence.

There was more to James Bond, as a character, than the unfulfilled dreams of Ian Fleming. Fleming stated that he based the character on several people he met during the war, and even 'M' shows signs of being based upon Godfrey with a similar impressive seafaring background. But let us not stray too far from the point: *Casino Royale* starts in a casino. Fleming was a big casino man before the war and compound that with his dream match against the Nazis you have the opening chapter – good verses evil at the gaming table.

Next, there is the direct correlation between Fleming's new fantasy world and the part of the Secret Service he knew first hand: the memo that opens chapter two.

It is widely said that much autobiography goes into a writer's first novel and Fleming certainly gives us enough evidence to demonstrate that he was at least writing about things he knew 'something of' from the war years. Memos of information/intelligence had to be turned into plans and operations eventually, and Fleming had a large hand in that construction; but not its implementation in the field. So again, enter Bond, the alter-ego that would take over.

To enforce this idea we learn of 'cipher' machines very early on in the text of *Casino Royale*, which allows us to make a direct comparison between Operation RUTHLESS (the capture of a super German cipher machine) and the novel.

RUTHLESS was one of Fleming's own operations that got shelved. So again, the frustration of not seeing something through or even being directly involved in dare-devil missions is highlighted.

Then there is the Japanese cipher analogy, which again, emanates from Fleming's trip to America and an introduction to SMERSH.

> '*SMERSH . . . remains today the most secret department of the soviet government.*'
>
> From Author's Note
> *From Russia With Love*

The creation of SMERSH has its origins in truth, as Fleming explained in his author's note to *From Russia With Love* (which some Bond fans consider to be his finest novel). In this novel you have the loyal figure of Felix Leiter, friendly CIA agent who assists Bond from time to time and who clearly has his roots in Fleming's trip to America during the war – the one he made directly after the Casino trip with Godfrey. The bomb explosion that occurs at the end of Chapter 5 in *Casino Royale* is also another real-life incident, as he confirmed in an inscribed copy of the book: 'the bomb trick was used by the Russians in an attempt on von Papen during the war in Ankara'.

Effectively, the first quarter of *Casino Royale* is based upon facts and real-life moments from Fleming's war experiences.

> '*. . . a young sapper who had earned his spurs as one of the secretariat to the Chiefs of Staff committee after being wounded during a sabotage operation in 1944, and had kept his sense of humour . . .*'

Could the above quote from the beginning of Chapter 3 of *Casino Royale* be a nod towards Captain Charles Drake, the senior officer in Room 39, who left the Royal Navy after a shell exploded in his face; or is it a reference to an unknown man from 30 Assault Unit who was injured on operational duty? A case of fact and fiction intertwining?

There are some snippets/nuances, not clearly defined within the first Bond thriller, that although have their origin during the Second World War, are more of a pastiche of what actually happened; indeed Bond himself is a pastiche. All the real-life heroes bled into one for Fleming. He genuinely hated desk jobs but never said he detested his time in Naval intelligence. He truly thought that he was doing something worthwhile there. Additionally, the job also did much to fulfil his own personal longing for adventure. Through Bond, Fleming was living his dream.

So what of the rest of *Casino Royale*?

It sails along with its own momentum. Fleming knew about Casinos – gambling – he knew the novel's location, he knew about beautiful women and dangerous agents, so the rest of the book wrote itself. But the list of ideas continued. Bond was a drug, the alter-ego Fleming needed, and so fourteen books rolled off the typewriter in approximately twelve years. That's a real cascade of ideas, especially when you consider the non-fiction, articles, interviews, films, and travelling – as well as socialising – Fleming did during that time. Fleming was prolific when it came to Bond, with two books even being published after his death.

So Fleming is fascinating to readers of novels because of the man he wanted to be; the man he so nearly could have been: James Bond. It is interesting to piece together the reality from within the fiction he created; but when one analyses it, it's almost like a conjuring trick explained away, it loses its magic. Do we really need to know that Mr Micawber was based upon Charles Dickens' father? Do we really need to know that Robin Hood never stole from the rich and gave to the poor? We will never be able to totally unravel the web of intricacy that Fleming based lots of Bond scenarios around. He was working in a top secret establishment and some of those secrets are nowadays lost forever. The one thing we are sure of is that Fleming's five years in Navy intelligence made such an impression on him, he wrote about it for virtually the rest of his life.

Chapter Sixteen

The Moonraker Affair

'The "realistic" spy tale takes some of the features of the genuine
spy world and exaggerates or exploits them. It portrays a universe
in which certain characteristics like friendliness and companionship
are absent and the qualities of loneliness and ambiguity of role
and motive are emphasised; a world in which both friend
and foe are outsiders, belonging to a professional
community with its own conventions.'

From Graham Greene's introduction to
The Spy's Bedside Book

This chapter is born out of a slight dissatisfaction with the
amount of evidence I found concerning 30 AU and the V.
Rocket campaigns. So I looked more clearly at this aspect of
their work in juxtaposition to Fleming's third novel,
Moonraker.

When I met some of the 30 AU veterans, I asked them
about their involvement in Operations CROSSBOW, BIG
BEN and PAPERCLIP. I asked about the occasional intelligence that filtered through concerning V rockets and was
told that there was a lot of work connected with the V1s and
V2s, that 30 AU had a specialist in Ralph Izzard who was so
important, his Number 2 was told to kill him if he fell into
enemy hands. I was also told that 30 AU had scientists
attached to their sections who were there solely to assess the
evidence of V rockets.

1. Commander Ian Fleming in Room 39 at the Admiralty. (*Times Newspapers Ltd*)

2. Patrick Dalzel-Job, 30 Assault Unit, probably the main inspiration for James Bond. (*Pen & Sword*)

3. Admiral Godfrey, quite possibly the original inspiration for 'M'. (*IWM*)

4. Staff Sergeant Bramah with Dalzel-Job. (*Pen & Sword*)

5. Charles Wheeler, 30 AU. (*Pen & Sword*)

6. Muriel Wright, Fleming's all-action girlfriend who died so tragically young. (*Times Newspapers Ltd*)

7. Joan Bright, friend of Fleming and secretary to Lord Ismay. (*Joan Bright*)

8. Squadron Leader Dennis Wheatley, the distinguished author and acquaintance of Ian Fleming.

9. Ron Guy of 30 AU who fell in love with a member of the French Resistance and was married soon after.

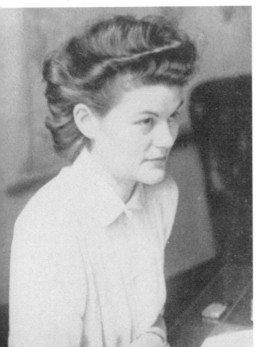

10. Unveiled Spring 2008, the 30 AU wall plaque for The Marine Public House, Littlehampton.

11. Official Naval Intelligence paper signed by Fleming with initial only and DNI designation 'NID 17' on signature block. (*National Archives*)

plan in greater detail with

rganisation and personnel.

mitted to C.C.O. for his

N.I.D.(17)
20.3.42.

12. Veterans of 30 AU, Bill Thomas and James Powell, at The Marine, Spring 2008. (*The author*)

So that is evidence directly sourced from the veterans concerning 30 AUs V rocket campaigns.

Then there is the evidence from Patrick Dalzel-Job's book *Arctic Snow to Dust of Normandy*. In this work he explained that it was early June 1944 that he took a squad of Royal Marines through a gap in enemy lines to seek out a V1 rocket site that had been identified by the RAF. He explained that his squad took a team of 'experts' to the site later that day (the scientists referred to by the veterans). The very day the first V1 fell on London.

The veterans also explained – and in slight contradiction to Dalzel-Job – that Fleming told 30 AU where the V rocket sites were located. They explained that he got his information through the French Resistance. We know that Dalzel-Job worked with the French Resistance, with some assistance from Staff-Sergeant Bramah, and said in his book that the French Resistance were dramatically underused during the war, but he used them, and Fleming apparently used them too.

None of the above is supposition. It is all first hand experience or first hand opinion from the people who were there. So we know categorically that Fleming/30 AU had something more than a passing interest in the V rocket campaigns towards the end of the Second World War.

Why is this important? Simply because if the most extreme rumours – that circulate around 30 AU – are correct, it was 30 AU who captured Wernher von Braun and Domberger in Bavaria at the end of the war. This I cannot substantiate, because if it is true it re-writes the history books and throws up many questions appertaining to the splitting up of Nazi scientists after the war (Operation PAPERCLIP). It is known that some scientists – including von Braun – went to American and worked on the rocket campaigns that led to NASA. It is known that some scientists went to Russia and started work on their rocket campaigns (and effectively started the space race and the 'superpowers'), and it is believed that 100 scientists worked for Britain under Operation SURGEON (a post-war program to exploit German aeronautics and deny German technical skills to Russia).

So how does this information work in relation to Ian Fleming and *Moonraker*?

In the novel there are effectively fifty Nazi scientists that work for Sir Hugo Drax in creating the Moonraker rocket. The rocket is described as a silver cigar-shaped missile, similar to the V2. The base for the rocket in the novel is the White Cliffs of Dover.

In reality 100 scientists who opted to work for Britain who used to work on the V rockets. Also, there are conspiracy theorists who believe that some scientists worked in chalk tunnels at Alum Bay, Isle of Wight, very similar to the White Cliffs of Dover in *Moonraker*. I don't believe this because a chalk tunnel from the fort above Alum Bay was cut many years before the Second World War and that is meant to be one of the clinching pieces of evidence in that theory. Also, it is known that Ian Fleming had to ask people about the scientific issues associated with the Moonraker in his novel, he didn't possess the information himself. This shows that if 30 AU had a real hands-on operation connected in some way to Operation PAPERCLIP or Operation SURGEON (no later than 1946), then Fleming probably didn't. Indeed he hung up his boots towards the end of 1945 before the main thrust of PAPERCLIP and, certainly before Operation SURGEON, kicked in.

What is interesting is the ground work laid down by Fleming from Operation CROSSBOW through to Operation BIG BEN. 30 AU received intelligence from Fleming we are told which he'd got from the French Resistance. We also know that the RAF supplied information. We know that Fleming studied aerial photographs. Clearly he must have worked through the SOE (Sir Colin Gubbins) to the Crossbow Committee, sharing his groundwork exercises, through 30 AU, to help the dive-bombing Spitfire missions that made up Operation BIG BEN.

It is for all this ground work, leading up to and including the first steps of Operation PAPERCLIP, that veterans of 30 AU thank Ian Fleming for. They say that the importance of stopping the V1s and V2s was tantamount to the success of the unit as a whole. The V rockets were the first terrorist attacks on London and a direct attack on civilian lives; 30 AU labour this point to this day. They took pride in the work they did at the coalface under all things V rocket related (they probably were not aware of the operational code words but certainly remember carrying out the tasks associated with them). They marvelled as to where Fleming got his intelligence from, because they maintain that he was right time after time. Then, in the next breath, they express their sadness that Fleming, despite all the work he did under this incredibly important operational requirement, was not credited for his major role countering the threat and closing the sites down (and arresting the scientists). But let us return to *Moonraker*. After James Bond thwarts Sir Hugo Drax's plan to blow up London with his Vengence-style rocket, Bond receives a thank you – through M – from the prime minister; but he receives no award (unlike the lady who worked with him). M reminds Bond that in their covert line of work, one doesn't receive those sought of awards (a George Cross in the novel). Does this scene emanate real-life for Fleming? It is difficult to tell. There is a distinct lack of evidence. I am using a blend of fact and fiction to make a plausible argument that Fleming and 30 AU played a significant part in Operations PAPERCLIP and SURGEON or, at least, laid significant foundations in Operations CROSSBOW and BIG BEN.

Veterans from 30 AU mention that most officers were decorated after the war who had operational duties in 30 AU. They also stated that certain parts of the unit didn't know what other parts were doing and now, with many veterans dead, their work is largely unappreciated. I certainly believe 30 AU and Ian Fleming had much to do with V rockets; I believe the evidence is there and I believe that they should get some credit for carrying out that most secret work.

To add more relevance to the comparison between *Moonraker* and Ian Fleming's Secret War, there are historical, albeit slightly fictionalised for Drax's sake, accounts of Otto Skorzeny's work. We know that Fleming was fascinated by Skorzeny and used his intelligence gathering commandos as a model for 30 AU. So there you have a comparison directly relevant to Fleming's 'Red Indians'. Skorzeny is mentioned by name in the book but I don't believe he was the model for Sir Hugo Drax, because Fleming makes Drax one of Skorzeny's men and his physical appearance is nothing like the real person, more like Aleister Crowley.

So through *Moonraker*, Fleming gives us the source of 30 AU, Nazi scientists, V rockets, all from a British, not American angle. There is also a brief mention of Russian technology in the form of a submarine that takes Drax away towards the end of the book.

> 'When I was lately talking over with Admiral Godfrey about the nature of Ian's wartime services, he summed it all up in a most memorable phrase, better I think than any laurel wreath or shining medal. "Ian," he said, "was a war-winner."'

> *Address given at the Memorial Service for*
> *Ian Fleming by William Plomer*
> St Bartholomew the Great, 15 September 1964

Chapter Seventeen

Love and War

'. . . there are two different ways of writing history: one is to
persuade men to virtue and the other is to compel men to truth.'

I, Claudius
Robert Graves

30 AU was not only one of Ian Fleming's greatest triumphs
during the Second World War, it was one of Great Britain's.
The speed, professionalism and secrecy in which the
various parts of the unit conducted its business was second
to none. They took great risks and accomplished so much
with – it appears – few fatalities.

The men of 30 AU were passionate about their work and
also something else: they were passionate about their love
lives too.

Patrick Dalzel-Job had fallen in love with a young lady
named Bjorg Bangsund who helped him on his little vessel
Mary Fortune before the war. He used to write to her
during the war through various people and took great
satisfaction in knowing that she was safe and away from
the fighting and, as soon as the war was over, he returned
to Norway (where he had left her), and they were reunited.
Dalzel-Job and Bjorg were married within three weeks
but Dalzel-Job was not the only one to find love.

If one ventures down to the 'Marine' public house in
Littlehampton, the blue-plaqued spiritual home of 30 AU,

there is a framed display on the wall depicting a painting of Royal Marine, Roy Guy. The painting is credited to Margot Guy and below the picture is a black and white photograph with a caption that states that Margot was a member of the French Resistance and she met Ron on 14 July 1944 near Vannes, France. They were later married in 1946 – the special relationship between the unit and the French Resistance got very special indeed!

But what about Ian Fleming? Did he have time for love with all early mornings, working lunches, and late nights he put in at the office?[121]

At the beginning of the war, Fleming was seeing Ann O'Neill, but he also had a deep affection for sporty Muriel Wright who was an air-raid warden. Fleming knew Muriel, or 'Honeytop' as he called her, before the war started. Muriel then became a despatch rider during the war but was killed, in March 1944 during an air raid, when a piece of masonry smashed through the window of her flat and smacked her on the head.

Muriel wasn't found straight away mainly because, as the building was still intact no-one believed that anyone was injured. But when Muriel's dog was found whimpering outside her apartment a full search was conducted and her body was found. Fleming was asked to identify the body, which he duly did. He then became filled with remorse for the girl who was so vibrant and beautiful and who he had treated so badly. What really brought things home to him was the fact that, just prior to her death, Muriel had popped out to buy his favourite cigarettes.

Fleming really didn't have as much respect for the women he loved as he should (he did have female friends such as Joan Bright who really enjoyed his company but the women he courted saw harsher side of him). Fleming wanted his girlfriends for sex and little else. In that respect he was the archetypical male chauvinist, using certain women as he saw fit, being very laconic – even cold towards them. One could argue that he had no time for women because of the war effort but that would be missing the point. Fleming clearly looked upon them as dirty or, dirtier than men; this low opinion could stem from his final days at Sandhurst in the early 1930s, where he was in love with a girl called Peggy Barnard. She had watched Ian at Sandhurst's annual sports day but afterwards was taken to a ball by a mysterious man, who was, she informed Ian, a 'long-standing arrangement'. Fleming begged her not to go but she refused to let the man down. So after sports day, Fleming went to Soho and found a tart and duly caught gonorrhoea. His mother was appalled and instantly booked him into a clinic but, as time went on, Fleming's mother deemed it a better idea that he resign from the military academy altogether. Thus ended any opportunity of becoming an officer in the British Army.

Perhaps Fleming blamed women for his loss of military career: if one hadn't gone off with another man . . . if the girl he slept with was cleaner . . . then maybe he could have led 30 AU from the front line instead of from a chair hundreds of miles away in Whitehall. It's an opinion that does hold water when one appreciates that – as we've seen during this book – Fleming desparately wanted to be at the front line of battle but was always turned down by Godfrey.

It is very easy to criticise people, to be judgemental. In fact it is an occupational hazard of any biographer or historian. I chose to give the last word to Joan Bright Astley, a true friend of Ian Fleming, who knew him during the war years and, right at the end of his life. She told me:

> 'I didn't get on with James Bond but my son adored him, so I took him along to see Ian, and this was not long before Ian died . . . We went along to Victoria Square. He looked a bit sad. A bit ill – he was ill – he looked lonely, the house was rather dark. The sun

never goes into those houses in that square. I don't know where his wife was – no idea; but he beckoned my son [Richard Astley], he was about fourteen at the time, over and said, "One of the best jobs you could do when you grow up is become a bursar on an ocean liner. You'll get to see the world". And I remember thinking to myself oh how boring, why couldn't he say something funny, because what he did say didn't make much sense at all. But that was very much Ian and those way out remarks I found so irritating because I could see no point in them. If you have a boy there you should say, "Listen chum, don't write books", or something like that.'

'Ian was more persuasive [than his brother Peter], had more apparent and vocal concern towards the people he liked, wanting them to do what he thought would be to their advantage; but he could also detach himself from them and temporarily but summarily dismiss them from his thoughts; he would return to them – or not – later, depending on how he felt, knowing they would be glad to have him back. We who were fond of him always were.'

Conclusion

Fleming's Secret Service

'I have only one word more – Do not believe a syllable
the newspapers say, or what you hear.
Mankind seems fond of telling lies.'

Lord Nelson
(letter to Emma Hamilton, HMS *Victory, 27 May 1804)*

All writers are influenced by the things that happen in their own lifetime; but unlike most, Fleming was not allowed to give away the intimate details of his work during the Second World War. So 007 was a world away from the reality Fleming was both part of and attached to during the war.

Fleming never wrote directly about real-life political issues. His villains were always on a post-war grand scale and, that's what keeps them fresh. Even though SMERSCH and the odd Russian spy lurk in dark corners, it is never rammed down our throats; James Bond doesn't adopt the Cold War genre, unlike some of the work of John Le Carre or, to a degree, Frederick Forsyth.

Ian Fleming's fantasy James Bond world allowed the British Secret Service – and all their foes – to live within a limitless expense budget. This has been faithfully translated to the big screen – well certainly, in expense budget terms anyway! In that sense the Bond films are faithful to the original stories: they exaggerate the truth, they are detached from reality. We consequently see the most expensive cars, locations, secret hideouts, gadgets and women! The reality of a true-to-life secret agent is living out in the elements in Norway, taking photographs of German convoys and then radioing back to base at regular intervals, then losing socks, back-packs, and slipping into ice-cold ponds; such was the day-to-day intelligence work of Patrick Dalzel-Job, before joining 30 AU, and outlined in his autobiography.

It is annoying and slightly frustrating to hear certain people declared the 'real James Bond'. He didn't exist, he was a pastiche. Unlike Sherlock Holmes who had a one-off counterpart in Sir Arthur Conan Doyle's medical past, Bond doesn't truly have that comparison. Again, this highlights the extra step Fleming took away from reality with regard to his creation. Bond's villains do have real-life counterparts though, namely, Le Chiffe, Blowfeld and Dr No, the former two possibly from Fleming's NID days.

Fleming would frequently draw from life and sometimes painstakingly get the detail right. This can be seen quite clearly in his friendship and reliance on Geoffrey Boothroyd – the man who became Q – with regard to small arms and the way they are used and explained in the Bond novels (with dramatic effect from *Dr No* onwards). This detail has been instrumental in 'playing up' the operational realism in the Bond stories, giving Fleming more authority as an informed writer. But, as it happens, this also highlights his lack of military training, operational experience and scientific knowledge (the latter clearly expressed in his research for *Moonraker*).

Fleming kept his Bond fantasies away from the realities he experienced in NID because those realities were desk-bound, albeit important, and sometimes laborious. His pragmatic mind and punchy prose was nurtured at Reuters and NID and often expounded at the dinner table. A good example of this latter trait is Fleming's dinner with President Kennedy. After the meal was over, Fleming related his ideas about how to discredit Fidel Castro. These ideas were reported to the CIA chief Allen Welsh Dulles, who reputedly gave the ideas serious consideration. All of this happened in March 1960 some fifteen years after Fleming had left NID; a leopard doesn't change its spots (just as Fleming hadn't with the *Diamond Smugglers* project).

Many people will come to this book because of their interest in the Second World War and the operational duties of Whitehall, but there will be many others who hope to glimpse, or take a whiff of, martinis shaken but not stirred. I have no problem with that. However, it is my duty to state that Britain's budget during the Second World War couldn't finance a real James Bond and, frankly, to this day, no government, could do so. When one talks about crack commandos and secret operations, it is very difficult not to use Bond comparisons and that frankly sums up most peoples' perception of Fleming during his lifetime.

Ian Fleming had two separate careers: his work as a Commander RNVR during the Second World War and his work as a writer of fictional spy stories. We should marvel and enjoy the legacy of both and, also, enjoy the juxtaposition of both careers too.

> 'All my life I have been interested in adventure, and, abroad, I have enjoyed the frisson of leaving the wide, well-lit streets and venturing up back alleys in search of the hidden, authentic pulse of towns . . . I had certainly got into the way of looking at people and places and things through a thriller-writer's eye.'
>
> *Thrilling Cities*
> Ian Fleming

Author's End Note

'The results were, to me, surprising and exciting.'
Stranger Than Fiction
Dennis Wheatley

I would like to conclude with a few observations concerning this book: readers may feel that I have gone a little over the top with endnotes/references in this work. I have done this deliberately because so much unsubstantiated theory has surrounded Fleming's work during the Second World War. I wanted to show the sheer weight of documented evidence that supports this work and my thought patterns. I am convinced that there is still more untold stories – possibly to do with Operations BIG BEN and PAPERCLIP – and that is an important point to note. For me it was important to 'speculate' in several areas (although I have discussed these areas thoroughly with veterans). I make no apology for that and it is clear where I have done so; but for the most part I have kept to the facts, using tried and proved documents and books wherever convenient, just to prove that Fleming's work was intricate and important.

I would like to state that although this book was first released during the Centenary year of Fleming's birth and acts as a compliment to his life's work – not just his work in NID – it was not the reason or excuse why I wrote the book in the first place. I find Fleming a wonderfully intriguing character and although I find his James Bond novels entertaining, I find his work during the Second World War more so. This book is something I wanted to write about aside from any significant anniversary. I did a similar thing with Dennis Wheatley before and, largely because of that book, found Wheatley again in this book.

Ian Fleming's contribution to the Allied fight during the Second World War wasn't the most significant but it was both useful and rewarding to him and to the British nation.

It is true that pure innovators are often overlooked or taken for granted because they cause so many waves flouting convention. In the music world Jerry Lee Lewis, John Lennon and David Bowie have proved this time and again over the past fifty years and people like Fleming and, to a degree, Dennis Wheatley have done the same in the literary world. And who replaces this calibre of men? The world is a self-healing wound when it comes to war, music and books – someone else will always crop up and sate the hunger of the initiated.

'Where is my Successor? I am not a little surprised at his not arriving!'

Lord Nelson
(letter to Emma Hamilton, HMS Victory,
23 November 1804)

Annexe A

National Archive References

I have included my official source documents as a stand alone Annexe in this book rather than a point ten aside somewhere at the back, in order to show the general reader the scope of the information that lies in the National Archive. I have by no means documented every nuance of the various operations detailed in the documentation (because of repetition and irrelevance in respect to the main subject matter of this book). However, if any reader wishes to explore the wealth of information to hand, clear indications of where to look are documented here via reference number and title (some titles are edited because of repetition or lack of space available).

All of the following files/papers/photos within the National Archive (at Kew) were studied as part of the research for this book. Some are included purely because they give so much information concerning such things as U-boat activity (from other parts of NID), not all feature directly the work of Ian Fleming but many do and, quite extensively too.

ADM 1/15798 – Admiralty, and Ministry of Defence, Navy Department, Correspondence and Papers.

Foreign Countries (53): Operation Woolforce: reports of activities of No 30 Assault Unit in Paris 1944.

ADM 199/2488 – Admiralty: War History Cases and
  Papers. Second World War. Director of Navy
  Intelligence . . . 30 Assault Unit documents and
  duplicates of port war damage information,
  including CX information.

ADM 202/308 – Admiralty and Ministry of Defence:
  Royal Marines: war diaries unit diaries, detachment
  reports and orders.

30 Assault Unit, Admiralty and Ministry of Defence.

ADM 202/598 – Admiralty and Ministry of Defence.

30 Assault Unit: Photographs vol 1.

World War II. Advance on Cherbourg. Surrender to 30
  Assault Unit, Royal Marines, or Naval headquarters
  personnel. Prisoners emerge from tunnel at
  Octeville, 26 June.

ADM 202/599 – Admiralty and Ministry of Defence.

30 Assault Unit vol 2: war diaries, unit diaries and
  detachment reports.

ADM 223/213 – Admiralty: Navy Intelligence Division
  and Operational Intelligence Centre: intelligence
  reports and papers.

Appendix 1 (part 5): History of SIGINT operations
  undertaken by 30 Commando/30 Assault Unit.

ADM 223/214 – Appendix 1 (part 5): History of 30
  Commando (later called 30 Assault Unit and 30
  Advanced Unit also known as Special Engineering
  Unit): includes part played by Commander Ian
  Fleming, Operation Torch (North Africa), Dieppe
  Raid, Operation Bantam (Calabria).

ADM 223/500 – 30 Assault Unit (formally Special
  Engineering Unit) and 30 Commando: papers,

including field information agency and technical. Also correspondence with Commander Ian Fleming, intelligence information and capture of weapons required for Operation Overlord (Normandy).

ADM 202/598 – 30 Assault Unit: photographs vol 1. 30 Assault Unit: photographs vol 1 Admiralty and Ministry of Defence . . .

ADM 202/599 – 30 Assault Unit vol 2. 30 Assault Unit, vol 2 Admiralty and Ministry of Defence . . .

ADM 223/464 – Admiralty: Navy Intelligence Division and Operational Intelligence Centre. Reports and Papers.

History of Naval Intelligence and the Naval Intelligence department 1939–45 including raids on Scharnhorst, Gneisenau and Graf Spee. Also operation Ruthless (capture of German Enigma cipher machine) planned by Commander Ian Fleming, Operation Husky . . .

ADM 223/480 – Admiralty: Naval Intelligence Division and Operational Intelligence Centre. Reports and papers.

U-boat supply ships at Cape Verde. Rubble (special steels and machine tools) contracts in Sweden . . . correspondence with Commander Ian Fleming.

ADM 223/490 – Admiralty: Naval Intelligence Division and Operational Intelligence Centre. Intelligence reports and papers.

Spain (including North Africa territories) and Portugal. Includes Goldeneye (precautions against German invasion of Spain) and correspondence with Commander Ian Fleming.

ADM 223/1 – Intelligence Reports and Papers U-boat methods of combined attack on convoys 1 Feb–31 Oct 1941.

ADM 223/2 – Admiralty Intelligence Papers.

ADM 223/3 – Admiralty Intelligence Papers 1941–42.

ADM 223/349 – Admiralty: Naval Intelligence Division and Operational Intelligence Centre: intelligence and reports.

No 30 Assault Unit: targets lists for operations in Germany (second edition).

ADM 223/501 – Admiralty: Navy Intelligence Division and Operational Intelligence Centre: intelligence reports and Papers.

30 Assault Unit targets Admiralty . . . reports and papers NID Volumes.

AIR 16/1266 – Tracking of Flight of Rudolf Hess.

AIR 20/5238 – Operation "Ruthless", deception to capture German air-sea rescue boat 17–26 October 1940.

Box 4 ACH/4 – African Coastal Flotilla: mostly research notes about units' operations during Second World War . . .

1705/15 – Negative sheet number 1/N20/31

Ian Fleming – author of the James Bond stories.

CSC 11/98 – Civil Service Commission: Recruitment and Establishment.

Ian Lancaster Fleming.

DEDE 2/1107 – Combined Operations Headquarters, and Ministry of Defence . . . Amphibious Warfare Headquarters.

30 Assault Unit (formally Special Engineering Unit, formally 30 Commando, later 30 Advanced Unit): mobilisation, control, disbandment, honours and awards.

FO 371/26565 – Flight of Rudolf Hess to Scotland.

FO 371/26566 – Flight of Rudolf Hess to Scotland.

FO 371/55930 – Connection of Albrect Haushofer with flight of Rudolf Hess.

HW 8/104 – Government Code and Cypher School: Naval Section: reports, working aids and correspondence.

History of 30 Commando (latterly called 30 Assault Unit and 30 Advance Unit) including History of SIGINT operations undertaken by 30 Commando/30 AU. This is a detailed account of wartime operations conducted by 30 Commando to obtain enemy documents and equipment.

IR 59/980 and IR 59/981 – Referenced as: Board of stamps: Legacy Duty Officer and successors: selection death duty accounts: Ian Fleming (no permission to view this document – listed here for reference purposes only).

WO219/1160 – War Office: Supreme Headquarters . . . 30 Assault Unit: miscellaneous cables . . .

X812/10/1 – Information relating to document.

Letter and copy of article, concerning the James Bond story *Dr No*, with letter from the author Ian Fleming (1958).

Annexe B

German Indications of Priority

It was deemed useful to have some detail concerning ciphers and the urgency of having them deciphered. The following document outlines the intricacies of the German cipher priority, which will give the reader a greater insight into the important traffic that travelled by cipher during the Second World War.

'24 June 1941

There has been considerable variations in the interpretations put on the letters used inside and outside cipher to indicate the degree of urgency; and this has led to some confusion in equating them with the terms laid down in "Signalling Instructions (SP 02201)."

The German indications are defined as follows:

FRE: – Message originated by the Führer or addressed to him.

KR: – Important war W/T messages: enemy reports; urgent messages from the Higher Command . . .

SSD: – Urgent messages concerning the movements of ships of war.

Authorised users are the same as for KR.

<u>S:</u> – Urgent messages of a military character (not administrative).

Authorised users are the same as for KR and SSD; and in addition Senior Officers and Directors of independently operating Headquarters and Depots.

Comparison with articles 129–130 of "Signalling Instructions" makes it clear that the priority-categories used in the Royal Navy do not correspond exactly with the German ones.'[122]

Annexe C

Astrology

The following information is extremely important with regard to British intelligences interest in astrology, especially with regard to the Rudolf Hess case. I can not rule out the possibility of a deep interest forming around the Nazis obsession with astrology and the occult, indeed so many strands of information suggest as much; the presence of Lois de Wohl also proves as much.

'During the Summer of 1940 DNI came into contact with Lois de Wohl, an Austro-Hungarian living in England, who had been studying astrology for twelve years. It had been known for some time that Hitler attached importance to astrological advice; the names of his advisors were known and that he had recently acquired the services of a Swiss, Branhuebuer. Because it is claimed that astrology is an exact science and leads reputable astrologers to the same conclusions, it seemed possible to ascertain what advice was, in fact, being offered to Hitler. On September 9th 1940, DNI sent a docket on this subject to the First Lord, the First Sea Lord and the VCNS. In it he pointed out that the significance of Hitler's astrological researches was not whether they were productive of the truth but that Hitler believed in them, and he concluded that this approach "might well be turned to practical use"'.

The DNI attached enough importance to this to suggest that "formation of a group of sincere astrologers prepared to work on these subjects is by no means a fantastic idea", and VCNS commented: "We might have a new department in NID." The [First] Sea Lord, perhaps not having clearly distinguished in his mind between what *is* true and what Hitler believed to be true, said: "Interesting, but I should like to work on something more solid than horoscopes", and Mr Alexander briefly agreed. It is worth remarking that Mr de Wohl emphasised September 15 1940 as the day on which, for a period, luck would turn against Hitler. "From Sep 15th on would have discouraging effect". On that day, 185 German aeroplanes were brought down. It was the turning point in the Battle of Britain.

Annexe D

SOE Teething Problems

The following document was written from a desk officer in NIDs point of view – Charles Morgan – regarding SOE. Morgan wrote up the history of NID and the following statement allows us to understand the frustrations with the then new department and allows us to speculate – from an informed point of view – how Fleming bridged the gag in experience between NID and SOE. Although the following document does not concern any activity Fleming had in 17 (it refers to the French sub-section of Section 1), it does show the problems NID was experiencing with the newly formed department.

In their book Gubbins and SOE *(Leo Cooper, 1993), Peter Wilkinson and Joan Bright Astley revealed more layers to SOE than hitherto been appreciated. Their work could be labelled sympathetic, especially in their treatment of Colin Gubbins – department head – because he and his department were not very well liked at the time (as depicted in the following document). However I do believe the problems with the department came down to an overall lack of experience and Fleming played his part in turning that around.*

I think perhaps Lord Selborne crystalised Gubbins and his section quite succinctly in a letter dated 17 October 1945: '... when a strong man [Gubbins] is fighting to create a new organization which had to be carved out of three services and other departments, it is not unnatural that he sometimes trod rather badly on people's toes.'

Fleming experienced exactly the same thing when creating 30

AU albeit out of different services and giving them their own remit, and working beside the regular army.

'SOE Teething Troubles

Early in the year the newly organised SOE became a thorn in the flesh. It was created to undertake the subversible activities which had formerly belonged to Section D of C's organisation, and, being very young, was a little blinded by the cloak and dazzled by the dagger. Its relations with C are not our concern, but its energies were for a time a source of considerable embarrassment to NID itself. At the time, heavy damage was being done to our trade by a few U-boat commanders. One of SOEs earliest enthusiasms was a scheme to collaborate with the friendly population of Brittany in assisting them. It all ended on paper, but not before the French sub-section of Section 1 had spent good hours of labour in pretending to take wild-cat seriously. Some time was to pass before the fierce young animal became house trained.'

I would be unfair to leave this Annexe on a negative note. Joan Bright had fond memories of SOE, as she explained to me: 'SOE was a marvellous place. MI6, MI5, SOE, there was a lot of jealousies and MI6 really didn't like the new group [SOE] . . . In the War Office we were concentrating on Resistance, Blockade and Propaganda; that's what we thought would win the war. My department MIR became SOE, because Churchill became inspired. His imagination wanted to set Europe ablaze. I didn't want to go into the SOE, so that was how I found my job working for General Ismay.'

But what about the jealousies? Joan explained, 'When you are doing secret work there is always jealousy because you are doing secret work!'

Proposal for Naval Intelligence Commando Unit

What follows is the original document written by Fleming concerning the formation of 30 Assault Unit. Interestingly he didn't envisage running the unit himself. The response to this memo came back from Godfrey and laid the future in tablets of stone (Godfrey's response is printed at the end of Fleming's document). These documents really crystallize what 30 Assault Unit would become and show clearly Fleming's talent for practical ideas based upon intelligence gained.

But it doesn't end there. On the 6 September 1970, Godfrey was asked to write a special file note to close – or rather open the file ADM 223/214 – that laid out the history of how 30 AU was formed[123]. This note concludes this Annexe (I have labelled each document One, Two and Three for clarity), which really showcases the vision, respect and success of Fleming's 'Red Indians.'

One:
Proposal for Naval Intelligence Commando Unit
i)   One of the most outstanding innovations in German intelligence is the creation by the German NID of Special Intelligence "Commandos" [Skorzeny's unit of commandos].

ii)   These "Commandos" accompany the forward troops when a port or naval installation is being attacked and, if the attack is successful their duty is to capture documents, cyphers [sic] etc. before these can be destroyed by the defenders.

iii) They have various other intelligence duties which are described in the attached memorandum [not attached].

I submit that we would do well to consider organising such a "Commando" within the NID, for use when we reassume the offensive on the continent, in Norway or elsewhere. The unit would be modelled on the same lines as its German counterpart and would be placed under the command of CCO perhaps a month before a specific objective is attacked.

Its duties would be.
To find out all NID sections' requirements from the port attacked, e.g. cyphers, specimens of material (including enemy oil fuel and food, for instance) charts, enemy fleet orders, mines, RDF gear, photographs etc etc.

Obtain all intelligence available as to where in the particular port these things would be found.

Train with raiding force.

Proceed with 2nd or 3rd wave of attacks into the port, and make straight for the various buildings etc. where the booty is expected to be found, capture it and return.

Operation "Sledgehammer" is a typical example of an objective which might yield valuable fruit if tackled by such a unit.

Propose:
I should submit the plan in greater detail with suggestions for organisation and personnel.

The principle be submitted to CCO for his covering approval.

[signed initial only] F.
NID (17)
20.3.42'

Two:
Godfrey's memo dated 13 April 42:

'. . . I think it would be a mistake to turn over the working out of an advance intelligence unit to the CCO . . . Moreover, that he and his Intelligence Staff are better able to work out such an arrangement than DNI DDNI and Section 17c. I should therefore like the matter to be tackled by Cdr Drake and Cdr Fleming under the supervision of DDNI who is requested to treat the matter as one of primary importance . . .'

Three:
30 AU Note by Godfrey dated 5.9.70
It is significant that after three years of war the principle of decentralisation had been so thoroughly accepted that such an important development as 30 AU could be launched, and sponsored by the Admiralty, with JIC blessing, and initiated by the DNI.

The JIC paper dated 25.6.1942 would have reached the Chiefs of Staff through the Ministry of Defence and JIC machinery, and presumably reached the First Sea Lord without the Board of Admiralty being consulted.

The driving force provided by Commander Ian Fleming, RNVR, the DNI's personal assistant, ensured rapid transit through the departments with the minimum red tape.

The story of this interesting and unique unit is well summarised in Volume III of the Naval Monographs, and needs no further embellishment by me twenty-eight years later.

A supplementary JIC paper dated 25.6.1942 draws attention to Commander Ian Fleming's contribution at the Admiralty end and throughout every phase of the operation.

For such a novel enterprise it is essential an officer with drive and imagination of the highest order is supervising matters at headquarters, and looking after the 'Whitehall front', which exists not only on the Treasury but in the Admiralty itself, although in a much less virulent form than in the War Office and Air Ministry.

The evidence of these papers shows that the naval officer was able to carry the civilian with him. Reading between the lines, and after twenty-five years it would seem that collaboration at levels was good, even very good considering the novelty of the idea.

The success of 30 AU operations depended largely on full use being made on the ISTD and of its branch the 'Contact Registry', and it is significant that both the ISTD, the Contact Section, 30 AU, and the Contact Registry were initiated, organised, paid for and run by the Admiralty, and not the War Office although their work mostly dealt with land warfare, and politico military objectives and people.

JHG
6.9.70[124]

Annexe F

Collecting Ian Fleming First Editions

'Do not believe what you read in novels or books about the war.
There is nothing worse.'

Casino Royale

I have included a full bibliography of Ian Fleming's books and their collectable variants so the reader can appreciate how extensive and sought-after Fleming's work is amongst serious book collectors today. A great many of his first editions demand thousands of pounds, in pristine condition, nowadays and the general enthusiast needs a detailed guide as to what collectables they may possess, or indeed, a guide as to what books they need to complete their collection.

Also, I feel it is important to print – as an Annexe – the full range of Fleming's work released during his lifetime to highlight the amount of material he produced in such a short space of time as an author. This has been largely unappreciated and highlights his most lucrative career, albeit at the end of his life, where he used his many skills and experiences to colour the world of both fiction and non-fiction. He was a prolific ideas man in NID and would put those ideas into memo and 'sell' through the Admiral to make a reality. It is also a largely unappreciated fact that Fleming was a huge collector of books, some of which he would use as reference works for his James Bond novels (it is not known if any captured 30 AU documents/books formed part of his library; especially those with no direct intelligence reference).

Fleming's personal library was indeed one of note. He started collecting books after a conversation with Percy Muir, a bookseller at Dulau's and Elkin Matthews. His intention was to collect first editions; but he soon became bored with that and started to collect 'books that marked milestones of progress ...'

Fleming had his new collection specially bound in black buckram fleece-lined boxes with an image of his bookplate on the cover. His collection included Albert Einstein's *Grundlage der allgemeinen Relativitasheorie* and other notables such as *Origin of Species*, *Mein Kampf* and, diversely Vol 1, No 1 of the *Radio Times* and also *Scouting for Boys* ...

Fleming created a significant 'history of western civilisation', focusing on science and technology. He was a major lender to the 1963 exhibition 'Printing and the Mind of Man'. Approximately 600 books from Fleming's collection are held in Lilly Library at Indiana University, Bloomington, Indiana, USA, which were purchased directly from Fleming's estate after his death. It was his wish that the collection should not be split up and, indeed, it is still preserved to this day. Rightly then, that we should honour his own bibliography at the end of this book, as it adds to the legacy of the man, in the books he has left behind.

Notes: books detailed in this guide are those published during Fleming's lifetime or, those books heavily influenced by him/written about him, shortly after his death. The exception being a small selection of movie related pieces and important biographies (please note, only the most collectable paperbacks are listed), and some of the more interesting articles/interviews (note not all articles and/or serialisations are listed because of space restrictions).

Please also note that the most collectable edition of each James Bond novel is the first edition, first issue, which always carries a price on the inside flap of the dustwrapper. Clipped copies and copies without a jacketed price are considered second issue and as a general rule: a price-sticker copy equates to a third issue (please see entries for first edition of *Octopussy* for clarity). Original prices and other issue points are included in their rightful place in the guide for clarity. Only meticulous details of boards, endpapers and precise details of books are given to James Bond first editions because of space available within this guide.

If readers have further queries concerning Fleming titles they are referred to antiquarian book dealers or, for general advice, a publication such as *Book and Magazine Collector* (available in most quality newsagents). Readers are asked not to contact the author or Pen & Sword Books for further information, as this information falls outside the remit of both.

JAMES BOND FIRST EDITIONS AND THEIR COLLECTABLE VARIANTS

Casino Royale, Jonathan Cape, first issue, (13 April 1953) first published 1953, no other printings mentioned on verso of title page, priced at 10s.6d on dustwrapper, rear panel of wrapper has pencil drawing of Ian Fleming by Bartlett and blurb about Fleming's life below it. Inner front flap of dustwrapper has blurb with jacket credit immediately below; rear flap is blank but for title, author, publisher and price in bottom left corner; black cloth boards with red heart to front board, plain endpapers, 218 pages. 4728 copies were bound up, a large number of which went to public libraries.

Casino Royale, Jonathan Cape, 1953, with second issue wrapper with *Times* review on front inner flap of dustwrapper.

Casino Royale (Pan, 1st p/back, 1955, first state with 2/- on cover).

Casino Royale (Pan, 1st p/back, 1955, second state with no price on cover).

Live and Let Die, Jonathan Cape, (5 May1954) 'First Published 1954' on verso title page (no other editions stated), plain white endpapers, 240 pages, rear flap of wrapper blank apart from price 10s. 6d, title and reviews of *Casino Royale*, first issue wrapper without credit to jacket designer Kenneth Lewis on front inner flap, black cloth, gilt lettering, emblem to front board. 7,500 copies were printed of the first edition

Live and Let Die, Jonathan Cape, 1954, second issue, priced 10s. 6d with two line credit to Kenneth Lewis midway between blurb and price on front inner flap of dust-wrapper.

Live and Let Die, Jonathan Cape, 1954, third issue, with two line credit to Kenneth Lewis directly below blurb on front inner flap.

Moonraker, Jonathan Cape, (7 April 1955) 'First Published 1955' verso title page (no other prints stated), plain white endpapers, 256 pages, black cloth, silver lettering, title to front board, priced 10s.6d on dust-wrapper. There is an issue point on page 10, last line 'shoot' instead of 'shoo' believed to be first issue (it is surmised that 'T' became dislodged during the print run as it was part of the same run not an issue point – 'shoot' is preferred). There are two text block thick-nesses, the first having a 19mm text block, which is the more desirable issue as not as prone to as much page browning and often thought to be better quality earlier variant of first issue but unsubstantiated. Front flap mentions *Casino Royale* and *Live and Let Die* plus jacket credit, rear flap blank but with price and title to corner, rear panel reviews of *Casino Royale* and *Live and Let Die.*

Moonraker, Jonathan Cape, 1955, priced 10s,6d, first issue, second paper thicknesses: text block measures 15mm and is the more prone to browning. The first print run for *Moonraker* was 9,900 copies.

Diamonds Are Forever, Jonathan Cape, (26 March 1956) 'First Published 1956' verso title page (no other editions mentioned). Blind stamped diagonals to front board, plain white endpapers, 257 pages, artist Pat Marriot uncredited on first edition; front flap blurb about book; rear flap Raymond Chandler quote and reviews for *Live and Let Die* and *Moonraker*; rear panel photo of author and blurb, priced 12s.6d on dustwrapper. The first print run was 14,700 copies.

From Russia, With Love, Jonathan Cape, (8 April 1957) 'First Published' 1957 verso title page (no other editions mentioned), plain white endpapers, 253 pages. Front flap of dustwrapper blurb about book, jacket credit and info on gun shown, plus price 13s.6d, rear flap is blank, rear panel has review for *Diamonds Are Forever*. 15,000 copies of the first edition printed.

From Russia, With Love (rejected first sheets text blocks sold to book club – true first with blue boards and dustwrapper; although officially released after standard Jonathan Cape issue, Jonathan Cape mentioned on title page on book club issue but book club mentioned on inner flap of dustwrapper, 1957).

Note: this variant can be bought for under £100 whilst the publisher's official version – detailed above – commands many hundreds of pounds in nice condition.

Dr No, Jonathan Cape, (31 March 1958) 'First Published 1958' verso title page with (no other editions mentioned), plain white endpapers, 256 pages, black cloth, silver lettering, Priced 13s.6d on front flap of dustwrapper with blurb about book, rear flap just has jacket credits, rear panel has reviews for *From Russia With Love*. Note: first issue boards of book *without* blind-stamped dancing girl on front board (first issue wrapper with Fleming's name in black on spine – second impression author's name written in white on spine). 20,000 copies of first edition were printed.

Dr No, Jonathan Cape, 1958, with dancing girl on front board and first issue wrapper. Note: although no preference has been given to the first state cloth – with/without dancing girl – the one without is deemed to be rarer; this variant sometimes appears for sale without dustwrapper.

Dr No, colour comic book version (DC Comics, USA).

Dr No, first film tie-in p/back, Pan Books, 1963.

Goldfinger, Jonathan Cape, (23 March 1959) 'First Published 1959' verso title page (no other editions mentioned), plain white endpapers, 318 pages, black cloth, gilt lettering. Skull blind-stamped to boards with gold-leaf coins for eyes; front flap of dust-wrapper has blurb about book and *Dr No* review, priced 15s, rear flap reviews of *The Diamond Smugglers*, rear panel reviews *From Russia, With Love* and all books down to *Casino Royale*. 25,000 copies were printed of the first edition.

Goldfinger, Jonathan Cape, 1959 – first edition with second issue wrapper, bevelled front flap without price.

Goldfinger (US Macmillan edition, bound and printed in Britain for US market one of 7,500 opposed to 28,000 UK dustwrapper).

Goldfinger (film tie-in p/back).

For Your Eyes Only, Jonathan Cape, (11 April 1960) First Published 1960 verso of title page (no other editions mentioned), plain endpapers, 252 pages; black cloth, silver lettering, white eye to front board, priced 15s on front flap of dustwrapper, blurb about book and *Goldfinger* review, rear flap reviews for *Diamond Smugglers* and *Dr No*, rear panel reviews *From Russia, With Love* down to *Casino Royale*. 21,712 copies of first edition printed.

Thunderball, Jonathan Cape, (27 March 1961) First Published 1961 verso title page (no other edition mentioned), black cloth, gilt lettering, blind stamped skeletal hand on front board; plain white endpapers, 254 pages, front flap of dustwrapper priced 15s, blurb about book and author, rear flap blurb about author continues, rear panel photograph of author. 50,938 copies of first edition printed.

The Spy Who Loved Me, Jonathan Cape, (16 April 1962) 'First Published 1962' verso title page, red endpapers, 221 pages, front flap of dustwrapper blurb by Vivienne Michel and priced 15s, rear flap blank, back panel review of *Thunderball*. Black cloth, silver lettering, silver dagger to front board (note: some copies do not have a gilt silver dagger on front board, just a blind-stamped dagger). 30,000 copies of first edition printed.

The Spy Who Loved Me, Jonathan Cape, 1962, with quad mark between 'E' and 'M' of Fleming's name on title page. This mark is not on the proof sheets and was just a spacer that worked loose during the print run; quad marked copies are scarcer and worth more than standard first edition.

On Her Majesty's Secret Service, Jonathan Cape, (1 April 1963) First Published 1963 verso title page (no other editions mentioned), white endpapers, 288 pages, black cloth, silver lettering, white swirl to front board (possibly signifying ski tracks), front flap blurb about the book, priced 16s, rear flap portrait of author and all previous titles, back panel reviews *Dr No, From*

Russia with Love, Thunderball, The Spy Who Loved Me. 45,000 copies of first edition printed.

On Her Majesty's Secret Service, Jonathan Cape, deluxe, ltd to 250 signed and numbered by the author, issued without dustwrapper.

On Her Majesty's Secret Service, Jonathan Cape, deluxe, ltd to 250 signed by author but *not* numbered – 43 copies only according to Cape's records, ten of which were given to Fleming, the rest intended as presentation copies.

You Only Live Twice, Jonathan Cape, (16 March 1964) First Published 1964 verso title page with no other editions mentioned, wood looking endpapers, black cloth, silver lettering, gilt Japanese letting to front board, front flap Japanese lettering and price 16s, rear flap all previous titles plus *Thrilling Cities, The Diamond Smugglers, All Night at Mr Stanyhurst's*, back panel continuation of art work and blurb. 56,000 copies of first edition printed.

You Only Live Twice, Jonathan Cape, 1964, has 'First Published March 1964' on verso of title page and therefore 2nd printing.

Note: there are two subtle shades of paper used for dustwrapper: one is pale green, one is pale brown. Neither are considered to be earlier than the other.

The Man With the Golden Gun, Jonathan Cape, (1 April 1965) First Published 1965 verso of title page and no other editions mentioned, green patterned endpapers, 221 pages, black cloth gilt lettering, front flap price 18s, title and 'the new James Bond', rear flap all previous titles and *Thrilling Cities, Diamond Smugglers, Chitty Chitty Bang Bang*, back panel continuation of artwork. Version with gold-block revolver on front boards of book is believed to be earliest variant of first edition, it was quickly withdrawn.

The Man With the Golden Gun, Jonathan Cape, 1965, without gold-blocked gun, 82,000 copies of first edition printed.

The Man With the Golden Gun, Jonathan Cape, 1965, without gold-blocked gun, but endpapers are white instead of green (these copies are deemed to be end of first print run, when green endpapers run out!).

Octopussy and The Living Daylights, Jonathan Cape, (23 June 1966) First Published 1966 verso title page with no other editions mentioned, gray marble patterned endpapers, 95 pages, black cloth, gilt lettering, front flap of dustwrapper lists all previous titles including *Thrilling Cities*, *The Diamond Smugglers*, *Chitty Chitty Bang Bang*, back panel author photograph. First issue dustwrapper has price 10s. 6d. 50,000 copies of first edition printed.

Octopussy and the Living Daylights, Jonathan Cape, 1966, second issue, no price on inner flap of wrapper, bevelled edge to flap is more prominent in second issue but it is not 'clipped' it was printed that way.

Octopussy and the Living Daylights, Jonathan Cape, 1966, third issue, price sticker on front inner flap of dustwrapper.

The Ivory Hammer (includes 'Property of a Lady') (first US, 1964)

Octopussy (Pan, first UK p/back includes first appearance of 'Property of a Lady' in a Bond anthology, 1st thus).

Octopussy and The Living Daylights (first UK issue to include '007 in New York', h/back, Viking, 2001)

OTHER BOND TITLES

Colonel Sun (Kingsley Amis as Robert Markham, Jonathan Cape, 1968, 21s on inner flap of dustwrapper).

(This title is included because it is rumoured, by some Bond fans, to be based upon some rough notes left by Fleming, but this has never been substantiated).

Note: a very unusual copy of *Colonel Sun* exists from Australia, with a striking Chinese devil's mask dust-wrapper. The book was issued by The Readers Book Club and numbered. It has 'Price in Australia, $2.65' and 'Members only 85s' on inner flap of dustwrapper.

CHILDREN'S BOOKS

Chitty-Chitty-Bang-Bang, the Magical Car: Adventure No. One (Jonathan Cape, 1964).

Chitty-Chitty-Bang-Bang, the Magical Car: Adventure No. Two (Jonathan Cape, 1964).

Chitty-Chitty-Bang-Bang, the Magical Car: Adventure No. Three (Jonathan Cape, 1964).

Chitty-Chitty-Bang-Bang (abridged for younger readers, I Can Read It All By Myself, 1965).

The Complete Adventures of the Magical Car (omnibus edition, Jonathan Cape, 1971).

NON-FICTION

The Diamond Smugglers (Jonathan Cape, 1957, gold writing to spine, early variant edition).

The Diamond Smugglers (Jonathan Cape, 1957, silver writing to spine, standard trade edition).

Thrilling Cities (Jonathan Cape, 1963).

Thrilling Cities (New American library, 1964, USA edition including '007 in New York').

Thrilling Cities (2 vol First issue UK p/back, Pan 1964).

Introducing Jamaica (Jonathan Cape, 1965).

Introducing Jamaica (Jonathan Cape, 1965, second issue with extra text issue point to top of dustwrapper).

UNIQUE EDITIONS

State of Excitement (one-off bound copy of book Fleming
  wrote about Kuwait in 1960)

PUBLISHER'S PROOF COPIES

Goldfinger (Jonathan Cape, 1959, proof).
Thunderball (Jonathan Cape, 1961, proof).
The Spy Who Loved Me (Jonathan Cape, 1962, proof).
On Her Majesty's Secret Service (Jonathan Cape, 1963,
  proof).
You Only Live Twice (Jonathan Cape, 1964, proof).
The Man With the Golden Gun (Jonathan Cape, 1965,
  proof).
Octopussy/The Living Daylights (Jonathan Cape, 1966,
  proof).
Colonel Sun (Jonathan Cape, 1967) (Robert Markham aka
  Kingsley Amis).
  Note: as a general rule: all publisher's proof copies are
p/back and have no illustration to front cover, just the title
of the book and white or off-yellow background design.

EARLY ANTHOLOGIES

Gilt Edged Bond (1st anthology, Macmillan, USA, 1961).
More Gilt Edged Bond (Macmillan, USA, 1965).

SPECIAL INTRODUCTIONS

The Education of a Poker Player (Jonathan Cape, 1959,
  Introduction only, 1959).
Airline Detective (Introduction only, Collins, 1962).
All Night at Mr Stannyhurst (by Hugh Edwards)
  (Introduction only by Ian Fleming, Jonathan Cape,
  1965).

CONTRIBUTIONS

The Kemsley Manual of Journalism (first book appearance of Fleming (USA, Cassell, 1950).

Spies Bedside Book (includes Ian and Peter Fleming, Rupert Hart-Davis, 1957) (There are three different colour cloths and no priority has been given to them as issue status).

Ditto with Introduction by Stella Rimington (Folio Society, 2006).

Ditto first trade edition with Introduction (Hutchinson, 2006).

Best Motoring Stories (compiled by John Welcome, Faber & Faber, 1959, includes Fleming's 'James Bond Dives', 1959).

Best Gambling Stories (compiled by John Welcome, Faber & Faber, 1961, includes Fleming's 'A Game of Bridge at Blades', 1961).

Motor Car Lovers Companion (edited by Richard Hough, George Allen & Unwin, 1965, includes Fleming, 1965).

Grand Slam Thirteen Bridge Stories (Bodley Head, 1975, includes Fleming's 'A Game of Bridge at Blades', 1975).

Note: a book possibly inspired the name of James Bond is *Birds of the West Indies* also by James Bond (Collins, 1936, 1947, 1960). This beautifully illustrated book is strongly collected by Ian Fleming enthusiasts and therefore demands a little more money on the collector's market than similar books in its series.

MAGAZINES

(Some Bond stories were originally serialised in *Playboy*), as follows:

Playboy March 1960 *The Hildebrand Rarity* (Bond short story published in *For Your Eyes Only*).

Playboy April-June 1963 *On Her Majesties Secret Service* (serialisation).

Playboy January 1964 *The Property of a Lady* (short story published in *Octopussy* from first paperback edition onwards).

Playboy April-June 1964 *You Only Live Twice* (serialisation).

Playboy December 1964 (Ian Fleming interview).

Playboy April-July 1965 *The Man With the Golden Gun* (serialisation).

Playboy November 1965 (Bond Girls cover story).

Playboy March-April 1966 *Octopussy* (serialisation).

(other Ian Fleming-related magazines).

Horizon Magazine (Dec 1947, 'Where Shall John Go' Fleming article).

Horizon Magazine (Dec 1949, Fleming article).

The Sunday Times, 11 September 1955, Fleming article 'The Great Riot of Istanbul'.

Holiday (April 1956, USA magazine, includes 'the Best Dining' article by Fleming).

Spectrum Extracts – Spectrum Extracts From The Spectator (1956) 'His Word His Bond'.

The Diamond Smugglers (articles) (*Sunday Times* Sep/Oct 1957).

Holiday (November 1960, USA magazine, includes article 'The Perplexing Date Line' by Fleming).

The Living Daylights (4 February 1962, *Sunday Times* Magazine).

The Guns of James Bond (true first edition, Sports Illustrated, US magazine, 19 March 1962).

The Guns of James Bond (later first UK edition in *Sunday Times* magazine, different illustrations to US counterpart, 18 November 1962).

Rogue, designed for men (April 1963, USA magazine including 'Dr Lobo of Macao' article by Ian Fleming, which eventually went into *Thrilling Cities*).

New York Herald Tribune (October 1963, includes 'Agent 007 in New York', which was later printed as '007 in New York' in the USA version of *Thrilling Cities* and the 2001 h/back UK Viking reprint of *Octopussy and The Living Daylights*).

Show, the magazine of the arts (November 1964, includes Ian Fleming's last interview).

The Book Collector, Spring 1965 (Percy Muir's article concerning why, how and from who Fleming acquired his extensive and most important book collection – considered to be a prime reference work and one of the most complete ever printed).

Sunday Times Magazine (15 August 1965, includes Ian Fleming's Jamaica, photography by Richard Steedman, one of Fleming's last ever articles).

Escape From Berlin (USA title of short story *The Living Daylights*, Intrigue Magazine, November 1965).

Life Magazine (7 Oct 1966, Part One 'Alias James Bond', US magazine with Fleming article cover story).

Life Magazine (14 October 1966, Part Two 'James Bond is Born', USA magazine, includes Sean Connery interview).

Note: During the 1960s the *Daily Express* ran a successful and long-running comic strip adaptation of the James Bond novels. Although Fleming didn't adapt the stories, they were nicely adapted illustrated alternative versions, which were reprinted in the 1980s and 1990s by Titan Books and are worthy of note.

MISCELLANEOUS

Holiday Book of the Worlds Fine Food (USA 1960, in slipcase).

Ian Fleming Memorial Service (5 September 1964, order of ceremony limited h/back edition with crepe wrap, restricted to 50 copies).

Ian Fleming Memorial Service (5 September 1964, order of ceremony, p/b with crepe wrap).

The James Bond Dossier (by Kingsley Amis, Jonathan Cape, 1965, h/back with dustwrapper).

For Bond Lovers Only (original paperback, Panther, 1965).

BIOGRAPHIES

The Life of Ian Fleming, Creator of James Bond by John Pearson (Jonathan Cape, 1966).

James Bond, the authorised biography by John Pearson (Sidgwick & Jackson, 1973).

Ian Fleming, the Man Behind James Bond by Andrew Lycett (first edition with priced wrapper, Weidenfeld & Nicolson, 1995).

Note (i): Fleming preserved his typed manuscripts in quarter morocco of various colours. His own copies of his books, many annotated, were bound in full morocco, also of various colours, and were not uniformly first editions.

The carbon typescript of *State of Excitement*, the one-off bound copy of book Fleming wrote about Kuwait in 1960. This was also bound in full red morocco (145 large quarto pages) by Sangorsi and Sutcliffe and resides in Lilly Library with other specially bound titles from this note.

RELATED MEMORABILIA

To kick off the Centenary celebrations for Ian Fleming, the Royal Mail released a set of stamps that can be obtained in many different collectable formats. Some of the main varieties are mentioned as follows:

Royal Mail Stamps – Ian Fleming's James Bond, 8 January 2008. Each individual stamp illustrates the covers from four first editions of the six featured books (Casino Royale, Dr No, Goldfinger, Diamonds Are Forever, For Your Eyes Only, From Russia With Love): the Jonathan Cape first edition, the UK paperback Pan edition, the US Jove paperback edition and the most recent Penguin paperback edition.

Presentation pack of mint stamps (some with '£50,000 in gold' mission card).

Traffic Light set of six mint stamps (unmounted mint).

Miniature sheet of mint stamps (unmounted mint).

Royal Mail Book of Stamps including first class stamps + Ian Fleming typewriter, James Bond Stamps and set of Ensign stamps (full colour with bio).

X2 First day Covers featuring set of stamps on one and miniature sheet on other, each with 'Ian Fleming 50 Years Dr No 1st Edition' postmark.

BFDC, Limited edition of 150 covers of James Bond stamps with 'Top Secret' 'Need to know', roulette wheel and typewriter depicted on front of each and limitation printed on reverse. 'Ian Fleming 50 Years Dr No 1st Edition' postmark.

First Day Cover special postmark with cocktail glass 'Ian Fleming Centenary, Bond Street, London W1, 8 January 2008'.

Mint set of PHQ Cards.

Used set of PHQ Cards 'Ian Fleming 50 Years Dr No 1st Edition' postmark (some sets with a set of stamps postmarked on additional PHQ card depicting the set).

Note: sets of PHQ cards with applicable stamps on them and posted without person's name on them on first day of issue. Almost impossible to get from dealers after issue day and are invariably extremely sort after, especially from specific literary of pop/rock related sets (such as *Lord of the Rings*, *Harry Potter* and *The Beatles*).

Second Note: there was two separate promotional items. The first was the Royal Mail 2008 pocket calendar, with front illustration of the James Bond stamps and details of the 2008 Royal Mail issues programme. Then there was the 2008 Royal Mail Stamp Guide, with front illustration of Bond Stamps and containing 4 pages of details about the James Bond issue project. Additionally, there were two point of sale A4 promotional full colour cards and one point of sale full colour poster.

Specialist First Day Covers

Bletchley Park, Limited edition cover numbered of 500 copies only, full colour 'Operation Ruthless' Top Secret theme.

Ian Fleming Publications Official Cover, with 'Ian Fleming Centenary' crest. The envelope also features artwork by Michael Gillette from the latest Penguin hardback edition of *Casino Royale* and quote from the original novel. '007' postmark.

The Stamp Centre, Black cover with Aston Martin DB4 illustration, Gold Dr No postmark and numbered '007' (when in fact it is the only one of its kind), with 'Ian Fleming Centenary' crest.

The Stamp Centre, Black cover with Aston Martin DB4 illustration, Silver Dr No postmark and declared a limited edition of 1,000 copies.

The Stamp Centre, Black cover with Aston Martin DB4 illustration, black postmark and numbered of 1,000 copies.

The Stamp Centre, Black cover with Aston Martin DB4 illustration, black postmark on miniature sheet and numbered of 250 copies.

Note: there is no gold or silver postmark on a miniature sheet cover in this set. Only four different covers exist and only one copy of the gold postmark variant.

The Stamp Centre, white cover with red thistle 'first day of issue' DPCPA standard post with 'Ian Fleming's James Bond Stamps on Sale 8 Jan' postmark with 'Ian Fleming centenary' crest and Benham PPK image postmark from Bond Street.

Note: some covers, because they were sent through standard post had inverted postmarks. These were withdrawn from sale, so copies of this variant are very scarce.

The Stamp Centre, white cover with 'first day cover Cotswold Covers' DPCPA standard post with 'Ian Fleming's James Bond Stamps on Sale 8 Jan' postmark with 'Ian Fleming centenary' crest and Benham PPK image postmark from Bond Street.

(*Note:* Stamp Centre confirmed to the author on 30 January 2008 that 950 was the eventual run of the black postmark limited edition.)

Note (ii): at the beginning of this annexe I mentioned that further information concerning Ian Fleming books can be gleaned from *Book and Magazine Collector*. This can be done through its letters page, but it is worth noting that prices for first editions – mainly of Bond titles – are updated frequently in regular articles, mostly appertaining to the last auction prices achieved.

Afterword

A Writer Not A Fighter

'And could you keep your heart in wonder at the daily miracles of
your life, your pain would seem less wondrous than your joy . . .'

The Prophet
Kahlil Gibran

This book has explored Ian Fleming's covert work during
the Second World War for NID and, although some of the
things he did were a revelation to him and others within
the echelons of His Majesty's government, there is no
doubting the significance of the work he did.

Of course, some may argue against that, but there was a
lot to be said for the work of NID, along with the Joint
Planning Staff of the Cabinet Office. The constant wave of
ideas and logical procession of creative thought was a real
inspiration for the CoS.

Fleming's literary work may have now passed into
legend, but Ian Fleming remains an iconic figure, not just
because of his pride and demeanour; but because his cease-
less drive and commitment to make things happen – as
highlighted here through the path of approximately five-
years of his life.

I believe Fleming's no-nonsense approach to life has cast
him in too poor a light in the modern day. Critics have
lacked perception and perspective and this has somewhat
tarnished the glittering triumphs of Ian Fleming: author

and esteemed veteran of naval intelligence. Let us now hope that this book has done something to polish his reputation and leave it bright and sparkling in the sports trophy cabinet of yesteryear. Over twenty successful Bond movies can't be wrong. The James Bond novels are not pulp fiction; but they are certainly treated the same way as science fiction or horror novels in the UK i.e. not seriously. Strange that the private detective novels of Raymond Chandler – a man who held Fleming in such high regard – are rated as better literature than Bond. Personally, I feel the reason for this is because Chandler's novels were a reflection of every day life, Bond was fantastical, an alter-ego one step removed from today. And that is an important point: you can't take Philip Marlowe out of his time and put him in present day; but you can take Bond. The reason why the Bond novels endure is because the detail of day-to-day life is covered in the glitz of Casino and exotic locale, which still exists.

> 'This is a true story about an author who was able to turn his natural imagination and storytelling genius to the fields of statecraft and strategy and to join in fellowship with those who were to become great.'
> From Air Marshal Sir Lawrence Darvall's
> introduction to *Stranger Than Fiction*
> Dennis Wheatley

For me, this is a sister work to my earlier book *Dennis Wheatley, Churchill's Storyteller*, which tells of the lateral thought of another top author of the twentieth century and the covert work he did for Whitehall during the Second World War. One reviewer said of that book that it was akin to Stephen King being asked by the president of the United States of America to help out with the War on Terror (well, Fleming did advise the President of the United States about a conflict, so not necessarily a leap of faith that one); and who is to say he couldn't turn up a few aces the so-called military experts hadn't? Creative thought is a dangerous thing. If we look back into the history of popular writing and look at the prophetic ideas of genre pioneers such as Jules Verne and H G Wells, one can marvel at the lack of foresight military personnel did have during the Great War – could Wells and Verne have helped them? Certainly not through rockets and time machines; but certainly through pioneering aircraft and submarines. It is the ideas that are important and, if one reads even segments of a book like *Shape of Things to Come*, the innovation, imagination and perception harnessed there impresses many people to this day. So to harp back to the beginning of this book to the idea of aloof writers, or at least all-too-serious perceptions of writers. These people – some, not all of them – do view the world from somewhere slightly outside of society. They can detach themselves and think laterally – see things others don't, because they beat the day-to-day system by sitting on their backside dreaming up great ideas. Another good example of this is Roald Dahl who, after his son had a road accident invented a head brace that no one in the medical world had before contemplated. In that capacity at least – the ability to harness lateral thought and imagination – writers show that the pen is indeed mightier than the sword. In Ian Fleming's case, he combined both planning and implementing vital war work with writing novels that are as loved today as when they were first published.

When we see – or at least sense – a piece of the Second World War in the Bond novels, we know that it goes back to an innovative moment in Fleming's war years, where a writer's imagination proved to be a voracious secret weapon.

'Long ago . . . I conceived the desire of writing a book. To scribble secretly and dream of authorship was one of my chief alleviations, and I read with a sympathetic envy every scrap I could get about the world of literature and the lives of literary people. It is something, even amidst this present happiness, to find leisure and opportunity to take up and partially realize these old and hopeless dreams. But that alone, in a world where so much of vivid and increasing interest presents itself to be done, even by an old man, would not, I think, suffice to set me at this desk . . .'

In the Days of the Comet
H G Wells

Bibliography

Actual editions used in research for this book are as follows (for National Archive details see Annexe A and also Text Notes detailed at the back of this book):

The truth about the Duke of Hamilton and the arrival of Rudolf Hess in Scotland. (Extract from Parliamentary Debates, House of Commons Official Records for the 22nd May, 1941, reproduced by permission of HM Stationery Office (original copy in Cabell Private Collection).

Original transcript of His Grace the 15th Duke of Hamilton's Statement Concerning Rudolf Hess (copy in Cabell Private Collection).

The Inner Circle, A View of War at the Top, Joan Bright Astley (Hutchinson, 1971).

Arctic Snow to Dust of Normandy, the Extraordinary Wartime Exploits of a Naval Special Agent, Patrick Dalzel-Job (new format edition) (Pen & Sword, 2005).

Soldier, the Autobiography of General Sir Mike Jackson (Bantam Press, 2007).

The Christopher Lee Filmography, all theatrical releases, 1948–2003, Tom Johnson and Mark A Miller (inscribed copy) (McFarland & Company, inc, Publishers, 1997).

Tall, Dark and Gruesome, Christopher Lee (publisher's proof copy and first Gollancz edition) (Victor Gollancz, 1997) .

Lord of Misrule, the autobiography of Christopher Lee (author's presentation copy, including original press release) (Orion, 2003).

The Life of Noel Coward, Cole Lesley (Jonathan Cape, 1976).

Ian Fleming, Andrew Lycett (Weidenfeld & Nicolson, 1995).

The Memoirs of Field Marshal the Viscount Montgomery of Alamein, KG (Collins, 1958).

The Flight of Rudolf Hess, Myth and Reality, Roy Conyers Nesbit and Georges Van Acker (Introduction by the Duke of Hamilton) (Sutton, 1999) .

Interrogations, the Nazi Elite in Allied Hands, 1945, Richard Overy (Allen Lane, The Penguin Press, 2001).

The Life of Ian Fleming, Creator of James Bond, by John Pearson (Jonathan Cape, 1966).

James Bond, the Authorised Biography (original promotional flyer), John Pearson (Jonathan Cape, 1973) .

Address Given at the Memorial Service for Ian Fleming by William Plomer, St Bartholomew the Great, September 15th 1964 (Westerham Press) (hardback and paperback used in research).

The Deceivers, Allied Military Deception in the Second World War, Thaddeus Holt (Weidenfeld & Nicholson, 2004).

Gubbins and SOE, Peter Wilkinson and Joan Bright Astley (Pen & Sword, 1993).

Room 39 – Naval Intelligence in Action 1939–45, Donald McLachlan (Weidenfeld & Nicholson, 1968).

Stranger Than Fiction, Dennis Wheatley (publisher's proof copy and inscribed first edition) (Hutchinson, 1959).

The Letters of Lord Nelson to Lady Hamilton . . . (2 vols) (Thomas Lovewell & Co, 1814) .

For Bond Lovers Only (various contributions) (Panther, 1965).

IAN FLEMING BOOKS USED IN RESEARCH:

Casino Royale (Daniel Craig film tie-in paperback).

Live and Let Die (1970s Pan re-issue).

Moonraker (1970s Pan re-issue).
Diamonds Are Forever (first UK edition).
From Russia, With Love (first UK edition).
Dr No (both variants of first UK edition).
Goldfinger (first UK edition).
For Your Eyes Only (1970s Pan re-issue).
Thunderball (first UK edition).
The Spy Who Loved Me (first UK edition).
On Her Majesties Secret Service (first UK edition).
You Only Live Twice (first UK edition).
The Man With the Golden Gun (first UK edition).
Octopussy and the Living Daylights (first UK edition and first UK
    paperback edition).
007 in New York (from Octopussy UK re-issue hardback).
Thrilling Cities (first UK edition and two-part first UK Pan).

MAGAZINE ARTICLES:

The Guns of James Bond by Ian Fleming (article, first US and first
    UK issues).
Life Magazine (7 Oct 1966, Part One 'Alias James Bond', US
    magazine with Fleming article cover story).
Life Magazine (14 October 1966, Part Two 'James Bond is Born',
    USA magazine, includes Sean Connery interview).

RECOMMENDED FURTHER READING

Those who wish to learn more about Ian Fleming's life, 30
    Assault Unit and British deception and military intelligence
    should read the following works:

*Arctic Snow to Dust of Normandy, the Exraordinary Wartime
    Exploits of a Naval Special Agent*, Patrick Dalzel-Job (Pen &
    Sword, 2005).
The History of 30 AU compiled by Gerald Hubert-Smith (ebook).
Beau Bete by Gerald Hubert-Smith (ebook).

Note: for either of the above books see
www.30au.co.uk/ianflemingsredindians.
The Hazard Mesh by J A Hugill (Hurst & Blackett, 1944).
Ian Fleming by Andrew Lycett (Weidenfeld & Nicolson, 1985).
Attain by Surprise edited by David Nutting (David Colver, 2003).

For those wishing a greater insight into Defence intelligence
during the Second World War, I suggest:
The Inner Circle: a view of war at the top by Joan Bright Astley
    (Hutchinson, 1971).
The Deceivers, Allied Military Deception in the Second World War
    by Thaddeus Holt (Weidenfeld & Nicolson, 2004).
Stranger Than Fiction by Dennis Wheatley (Hutchinson, 1959).

ORIGINAL INTERVIEWS

Christopher Lee (1997).
James 'Bill' Powell and Bill Thomas, *The Commando* Public
    House, Littlehampton (11 February 2008).
Joan Bright Astley OBE (27 February 2008).

About the Author

Craig Cabell is the writer of twelve previous books including *Dennis Wheatley – Churchill's Storyteller, Operation Big Ben – the anti-V2 Spitfire Missions 1944–45* (with Graham A. Thomas) and *VE Day – A Day to Remember* (with Allan Richards). Segments of his VE Day book has been acted on stage by Richard E Grant and serialised in the National Press. He has been a short story writer for radio, provided research material for radio and TV historical documentaries and interviewed princes, arms dealers and politicians. He is an advisor of rare and antiquarian books, from Charles Dickens to Ian Rankin, and has written countless articles and rare price guides for *Book and Magazine Collector*. For five years he was an in-house reporter with MOD *Focus*, where he wrote news, features, historical pieces and a regular wine column. He worked in the MoD press directorate during the second Gulf War and was one of the few people to speak in-depth to famous war veterans, such as Spike Milligan, about battle fatigue. Aside from this, he has been a freelance reporter for nearly twenty years, writing most notably for *The Independent* newspaper. He spent a happy year in his early-twenties working at the Admiralty, where he heard many interesting stories about the famous building: from the ghost of Lord Nelson to the formation of NID. He has also studied South America and the Caribbean in some depth, making various trips there for government services and actually handled Lord Nelson's telescope – aboard a Royal Navy vessel in the very port where the admiral once spied on the Spanish fleet under cover of darkness. Craig has also travelled to the Middle East and various parts of Europe in his line of duty. He is married with three children and has too many books in his ever expanding library.

Coming soon . . .
Ian Fleming's Red Indians – The History of 30 Assault Unit.

An account of the crack team of Commandos formed by Ian Fleming and dubbed his 'Red Indians' by the author himself.

30 AU conducted deep penetration exercises into occupied Europe to gather intelligence and sabotage secret Nazi bases, including one of the first V1 launch sites.

Taken from official archive documents and first-hand interviews with the members of the unit, *Ian Fleming's Red Indians*, is an exciting story of bravery and covert operations that will appeal to both historians and Ian Fleming fans alike. It shows the real-life counterparts to many 'mission impossible' exercises, as depicted in novel and cinema over the years. Read the exhilarating truth behind once covert stories that are still largely overlooked today.

Text Notes

1. Brother of senior partner in stockbroker firm Rowe and Pitman where Fleming was working at the time (see also note iv).
2. Rear Admiral John H Godfrey succeeded Rear Admiral Troup as Director of Naval Intelligence on 24 January 1939. It was recognised that war was inevitable and near, even at that stage. His immediate objective was to make preparations for it that were 'practical and imaginative' (ADM 223/464 refers).
3. Norman knew of Fleming through Bernard Rickatson-Hatt, who was Fleming's boss at Reuters in the early 1930s.
4. Lancelot 'Lancy' Hugh Smith was a senior partner of Rowe and Pitman. His brother Aubrey had been Deputy Director of Naval Intelligence during the Great War. Also Rowe and Pitman had many personnel who had worked in intelligence, including Claud Serocold, who was personal assistant to Admiral Hall during the Great War. It is also interesting that an unpublished official history of Rowe and Pitman said, 'It is interesting to speculate whether R&P's Lancelot Hugh Smith was, by his own involvement and through the medium of his brother, a long-term talent spotter for British Intelligence.' Wheels within wheels certainly brought Fleming to Admiral Godfrey's attention.
5. Fleming was thirty-one years of age at the time, so not a 'green' youth.

6. See *The Life of Ian Fleming, Creator of James Bond* by John Pearson (Jonathan Cape, 1966).
7. The following letter was sourced by John Pearson for his book *The Life of Ian Fleming, Creator of James Bond.*
8. An important point to note is: it was deemed by the Admiralty that as war commenced, Fleet's demand for active RN staff would increase, so it was therefore DNIs duty to ensure that there was some 'civilian dilution from the outset'. Of this fundamental principle Godfrey was deemed a pioneer amongst Naval staff (ADM 223/464).
9. 26 July 1939.
10. See ADM 223/464.
11. Fleming would be promoted to commander on 8 September.
12. From 1937 Fleming became interested in the growing Nazi threat and wrote an article and report concerning them. He sent the report to the British Embassy in Berlin; those wishing more details concerning Fleming's life during this period are referred to Andrew Lycett's biography *Ian Fleming* (Weldenfeld & Nicolson, 1995), as the information falls outside the remit of this book.
13. Ian was the second eldest of four brothers: Peter the eldest, who worked in British intelligence, the third, Richard, who served in the Lovat Scouts and the Seaforth Highlanders, who was wounded and received the Military Cross. And Michael, who died of wounds as a prisoner of the Nazis in 1940.
14. From an interview conducted by Craig Cabell in 1997.
15. See Christopher Lee's autobiography *Lord of Misrue* (Orion, 2003).
16. Johnson and Miller (McFarland & Company inc, 1994).
17. See *For Bond Lovers Only* (Panther, 1965).
18. Words of an unknown officer who spoke to John Pearson when he compiled his biography *The Life of Ian Fleming, Creator of James Bond* (Jonathan Cape, 1966).

19. In her book *The Inner Circle, A View of War at the Top* (Hutchinson, 1971), Joan spoke quite revealingly about both Ian and Peter Fleming: 'They were an attractive pair, amusing, good-looking, sure of themselves, and devoted to each other.'

20. Christopher Lee's autobiography was issued twice as *Tall, Dark and Gruesome*, in the late 1970s and late 90s (1997) respectively, the book was re-issued as *Lord of Misrule* (Orion, 2003). Lee's Fleming reminiscences appear in all versions of his autobiography.

21. Raymond Chandler in conversation with Donald Gomery and sourced from *For Bond Lovers Only* (Panther, 1965).

22. ADM 223/464, Enclosure 145, (co-ordination and special intelligence by C Morgan).

23. A man who would set up the propaganda cell in Room 39. However, interestingly, Delmer was previously known to Fleming as he had visited Russia with him as a fellow journalist, in March 1939.

24. The author of this book worked at the Admiralty for a year before RN was relocated to Victory Building, Portsmouth, in 1993. Much of the original building was still intact at the time, with its maze of 'below-street level' corridors and rooms, which the author was extremely familiar with.

25. As NID was codenamed 17, each desk within it took a letter of the alphabet after it, 17A, 17B, 17C, etc., Fleming being 17F.

26. Some people have speculated that Fleming based James Bond on Godfrey. The answer is no, as Donald McLahlan (fellow Room 39 officer) quoted Fleming as stating (see *For Bond Lovers Only*): 'Although he is almost a product of my imagination, I used various people I came across during the war – secret service men, commandos, newspaper men – as a basis for him. My experiences during the war, and my knowledge of intelligence work led me to write about them in a highly bowdlerized way, and I simply used Bond

as a central figure.' The character of M was far more fitting, as both M and Godfrey's last command were on HMS *Repulse* and both shared a taste for Algerian wine.

27. For clarity: on 1 January 1941 Lieutenant Donald McLachlan joined Section 1 of NID. Ten months later he was to start a section as 17Z, to treat subversion propaganda in Germany from the Naval point of view. Meanwhile, he worked on political matters within the main organisation of Section 1 and read and analysed special intelligence.

28. Note the (special), which stood for Special Operations. This corralates with the aforementioned RNVSR of Commander Bond in *Moonraker*. So a little of Fleming is Bond? Of course, he was the author and something had to shine through.

29. See Chapter XXV, *Dennis Wheatley - Churchill's Storyteller* by Craig Cabell (Spellmount, 2006) for a complete breakdown of the genesis of the operation, which started out as 'MINCEMEAT' (a very Wheatley-influenced code name). The London Controlling Section (LCS) of the War Cabinet along with Flight Lieutenant Chumley of MI5 conceived the operation and escalated the idea to Montagu. Why Chumley never complained is a mystery, however, before *The Man Who Never Was* was published, a book entitled *Operation Heartbreak* by Duff Cooper, Minister for Security, was released and criticised as a huge security breach. What with Chumley's sensitive day job, he probably didn't want any unnecessary publicity and therefore his important role is largely overlooked.

30. *Arctic Snow to Dust of Normandy, the Extraordinary Wartime Exploits of a Naval Special Agent,* Patrick Dalzel-Job (Pen & Sword, 2005).

31. Dalzel-Job would also comment in his autobiography 'He [Fleming] was quite kind to me, but somewhat cold and austere.' This, in a sense, shows the divide between the two men.

32. See Annexe B for a memo concerning the different way the German Navy treated ciphers. It shows the level of importance the RN gave to understanding the enemy intelligence.
33. See ADM 223/464.
34. See ADM 223/464
35. ADM 223/464 (enclosure 264).
36. This document originates from AIR 20/5238 and presented in my own format (but with no alteration to the narrative).
37. ADM 223/464 (enclosure 264).
38. The dreaming up of fantastic ideas was better placed with Bevan's team at the JPS.
39. There is a great amount of documentation within the National Archive concerning other parts of NID. There are thousands of pages devoted to shipping, U-boat sightings and operational duties. It was a real hive of activity. It must be stressed that I am concentrating not only on one part of the department, but essentially one man within it.
40. This information was sourced from original documentation detailed in ADM 223/464 enclosure 145 (see Annexe A).
41. This does sometimes provide frustration for the researcher as there is a natural leap between certain documents (due to an undocumented meeting/discussion that was important in the evolution of the work/operation in hand). This frustration is further enhanced by the absence of detailed background notes, which have to be sourced from other areas.
42. Many of the minutes of JPS meetings in the National Archive touch upon many operations from other departments, such as Operation GOLDENEYE, to name but one. It seems clear from this documentation that Fleming's work had a particular interest to the JPS.
43. Mason was the first statutory professor of Geography at Oxford University. His survey of the Himalayers in the

1920s rewarded him with a Royal Geographic Founders Medal. He was an intelligence officer in the Black Watch achieving the rank of Brevat-major. He was three times mentioned in dispatches.

44. Mason together with a combined academic team from Oxford and Cambridge produced the British Naval Intelligence Division Geographical Handbook Series (1941–46). 58 volumes were produced. These were books used by the Armed Forces engaged in military operations. Speed and accuracy were very important.

45. I have not found any evidence of such a visit in UK-based documentation and can draw the conclusion that people maybe getting confused between 'Station X' and 'Camp X'.

46. In his autobiography Sir Edward Heath mentioned brushing shoulders with Hitler and being aware of the might of the Nazi Party from the mid-1930s (this was also confirmed to the author in a subsequent interview). Also see the work of John Lewes concerning Jock Lewes (co-founder of the SAS).

47. When GOLDENEYE was mentioned during JPS meetings, it was described as a sound idea and not worthy of much discussion (which is almost an endorsement of its importance). GOLDENEYE, in fairness, fell quite strongly into NIDs lap as it was all about securing shipping lines and countermeasure if Gibraltar was lost (with Gibraltar being of huge significance to the RN): so radically Navy not JPS.

48. Operation TRACER would involve keeping a crack team of individuals secreted in a sealed room, albeit with observation points and radio contact, during enemy occupation of Gibraltar. This would feed important shipping intelligence back to the Royal Navy along with the day-to-day work of the enemy above.

49. Hillgarth also wrote thrillers, so not surprising then that Fleming liked him; but Hillgarth would scupper Operation GOLDENEYE somewhat.

50. During the first month of the Second World War, Hillgarth sent a top Spanish agent to London to acquire funds to purchase 55 German ships that resided in Spanish ports to stop them being used in the war effort. Godfrey liked this idea and engaged with people in the City – including Sir Edward Peacock – to mastermind a strategy of purchase. They came up with the idea of setting up a Spanish company that would purchase the ships with British money. Sir Andrew Duncan (Ministry of Transport) was against it, but in February 1940 Fleming pushed for a decision and the ships were bought.

51. Dr Cooper gave a first hand account to discovergibraltar.com in November 2006, aged 92. Further insight into this operation and Dr Cooper can be read at this website.

52. Godfrey and his successor ensured that when quality time was spent on worthwhile operations, it would be written up and turned into a user manual. For example, there was a small manual written about the crucial pointers to take into consideration when forming an Intelligence Assault Unit. When one reads the document, one can quickly see Fleming's mindset; indeed the manual is endorsed by Godfrey.

53. Roy Conyers Nesbit and George Van Acker wrote in *The Flight of Rudolf Hess, Myths and Reality* (Sutton, 1999) that there was nothing more to write about the subject. Hess made the decision to come to the UK himself. They include a two and a half page piece explaining away any ploy by British Intelligence to induce Hess to make the flight. However, the research they use still leaves me much pause for thought, and I hereby present my version of what could have happened.

54. In *The Spy's Bedside Book*, by Hugh and Graham Greene (Rupert Hart-Davis, 1957), there are some interesting segments from Peter Fleming's *Invasion 1940* (Rupert Hart-Davis, 1957), such as: 'Dr Herman Goertz, a lieutenant on

the reserve of the Luftwaffe, was dropped by parachute in County Meath on the night of 5/6 May 1940.' It appears that the landing of Nazis in the UK was something of interest to Peter Fleming albeit in a light-hearted way.

55. Interestingly, in Chapter One of *Diamonds Are Forever*, a secret flight takes place – albeit by helicopter – by a former Nazi pilot who flies one night in three during the year because of the full moon (astrology may figure strongly in Hess's flight).

56. Correspondence with Wing Commander C H Maclean, September/October (Nesbit Archives); sourced from *The Flight of Rudolf Hess, Myths and Reality* by Roy Conyers Nesbit and Georges Van Acker, with an Introduction by the [current] Duke of Hamilton (Sutton,1999). Cabell interviewed the duke on publication of the book at his estate in Scotland and was presented with some documentation, including an original hansard concerning Hess/Hamilton, which he has drawn from in the construction of the Hess chapter in this book.

57. See also 'The Truth about the Duke and the Arrival of Rudolf Hess in Scotland' 'Extract from Parliamentary Debates, House of Commons Official Reports for the 22nd May, 1941, reproduced by permission of HM Stationery Office.'

58. Albrecht later wrote, 'As the final possibility, I [mentioned] that a personal meeting on neutral soil with the closest of my English friends, the young Duke of Hamilton, who has access at all times to all important persons in London, even to Churchill and the king.' (source Duke of Hamilton)

59. I personally believe that this is the most important piece of information. Hess trusted Albrecht Haushofer and there must have been some serious planning by Hess and Haushofer (and some convincing mail from the UK) to send Hess on his way, which is why I cannot believe that Haushofer acted as a double-agent (it cannot be ruled out but I don't believe it), British intelligence instigated the

'trip' (which falls in line with the last text note (above) from the Duke of Hamilton's transcript of events). Haushofer, although opposed to the Nazi couldn't – I believe – double-cross his friend, so that leaves British Intelligence as the instigators.

60. Colville was a friend of Ian Fleming and had even spent a weekend with him and another shortly before Chamberlain's resignation. Fleming would also know Sir Alexander Cadogen and Ivor Kirkpatrick too in relation to his work.

61. When Churchill later met Stalin he was congratulated on luring Rudolf Hess to the UK. Churchill told him in no uncertain terms that the British government knew nothing of Hess's flight in advance.

62. There was a cartoon in *The Inquirer* dated 13 May 1941 about Peter's novel. The piece depicts Hess landing by parachute with the caption, 'And it's my guess that Hitler got a copy of this book and decided to try the idea out – with No3 man instead of himself'.

63. The detail of Hess, Colville and the Duke of Hamilton is taken from *The Flight of Rudolf Hess* by Roy Conyers Nesbit and Georges Van Acker (Sutton, 1999)

64. Albrecht Georg Hushofer was a significant influence on British intelligence during the Second World War. He was born on 7 January 1903 and was killed by the Gestapo on 23 April 1945. He was the son of General Professor Dr Karl Hushofer, a German geopolitician, which Albrecht became himself. He studied at Munich University under his father and alongside Rudolf Hess. After Hess's imprisonment of 1923 Albrecht was a frequent visitor of the future deputy fuehrer at Landsberg Prison. In 1931, he became Hess's advisor on foreign affairs, and although apposed to Nazi policies, was an advocate of German foreign policy throughout the 1930s. At the beginning of the Second World War Albrecht was part of Hitler's attempt to negotiate peace with the French and British. Albrecht fell on

hard times after Rudolf Hess's flight and was eventually arrested by the Gestapo in December 1944 after the Hitler bomb-plot failed, of which he was part.

65. See Annexe D for an enlightening look into the teething problems of the SOE, shortly after they were formed; which may explain why Fleming was very active with them (in a supporting role). ADM 223/464, Enclosure 257 refers.

66. Letter as laid down in *The Life of Ian Fleming, Creator of James Bond* by John Pearson (Jonathan Cape, 1966).

67. The Link was founded in 1937 by Admiral Barry Domvile and boasted some 4,300 members by June 1937. Its aim was 'to foster the mutual knowledge and understanding between the British and German peoples, and to counter-act the flood of lies with which our people were being regaled in their daily papers.' The Link also published its own journal *The Anglo-German Review*. The organisation was closed down in 1940.

68. Admiral Sir Barry Edward Domvile, was a distinguished Royal Navy officer who turned into a leading British fascist. Due to his pro-Nazi views, Domvile was interned during the Second World War under Defence Regulations 18B from 7 July 1940 to 29 July 1943. His diaries are held in the National Maritime Museum.

69. What I also find of interest is the fact that Operation Foxley was still being formed when the Hitler bomb plot occurred, which included Albrecht Haushofer.

70. During the writing of this book I interviewed Joan Bright who knew the Flemings and Wheatley well during the war. She mentioned that she/people who worked with secret material, never spoke about it to each other if it had nothing to do with them. I mentioned my Hess theory including the Flemings and Wheatley, she said 'I wouldn't know. It wasn't something you asked. Yes, there were secrets when it came to D Day, it was the secretaries who were the first to know the date of when it was going to

happen.' I asked her about *The Flying Visit*, she said, 'It was extraordinary that he should have written that. All from his own imagination. He gave me a copy of the book at the time as we were working in the same branch of the war office.'

71. Rudolf Hess's last flight fits so tantalisingly snug behind this last date in a possible period of good luck for Hitler. Also, the exact date – according to some sources – coincided with a very rare alignment of the planets, which Hess would definitely take as a good omen. If this is true and the theory of British Intelligence luring Hess to UK is true, the date would have had to be picked in consultation with experts such as de Wohl or Aleister Crowley (and possibly Fleming and Dennis Wheatley too).

72. For clarity, Tricycle was the codename of Dunstan 'Dusko' Popov, an extravagant Serbian playboy (allegedly named the Tricycle for his three in a bed romps; it is also believed that Fleming could have based 007's playboy/double agent life-style partly on Popov). Tricycle was also the name of a spy network Popov was part of. He was born in 1912 and died in 1981: he published his memoirs in 1974 entitled *Spy Counter-spy*. Stapleton would have known about Tricycle and in June/July Hoover was aware of the success of double agents in certain 'stings' as Holt described them. Hoover didn't really trust Tricycle, vindicated, shortly afterwards, when the British fell out with him too.

73. Sir William Samuel Stephenson (23 January 1897–31 January 1989) was a Canadian soldier, airman, businessman and head of the British Security Coordination (BSC) during the Second World War, where he was sent on 21 June 1940 by Winston Churchill himself. His codename was Intrepid.

74. Set up by MI6 in May 1940, the British Security Coordination (BSC) worked out of New York and was established to promote British Intelligence and Propaganda interests in the US. It was situated in Room

3603 in the Rockefeller Centre and headed by Canadian industrialist William Stephenson. The department fed important intelligence to MI5, MI6, SIS, SOE and PWE.

75. It is mentioned in Thaddeus Holt's book *The Deceivers, Allied Military Deception in the Second World War* that Godfrey's main reason for going to the USA was in connection with the 'Tricycle affair'.

76. ADM 223/464 refers to the USA trip of Godfrey and Fleming, noting a month after the duo arrived: 'A Joint Staff Mission was sent to Washington in June 1941 to discuss what role USA would have if they joined the war. DNI was in US at that time with a view to lecture about security on big navy ports (this was suggested to DNI by Colonel Neville).' There was however much more to Godfrey and Fleming's trip than that.

77. This could well have included Tricycle or people connected with him and even people like Hushofer.

78. It was here that Fleming met up with his brother and Joan Bright briefly, although Ian soon 'disappeared' as Joan later recalled in her book *The Inner Circle, A View of War at the Top* (Hutchinson, 1971).

79. Relations between US and UK did sometimes breakdown due to problems with the way the British conducted their intelligence work in-country. Sometimes this was definitely the fault of the British for doing things in a slightly underhanded way; other times it was down to J Edgar Hoover and his bloody-minded approach to sharing with the British.

80. Strangely, in his non-fiction *Thrilling Cities*, Fleming is not over-complimentary about Americans. In fact, when covering New York he is most uncharitable at times, which probably accounts for a very short James Bond story in the US edition of the book; printed at the end of the chapter, which only found its way into UK hardback at the turn of the Millennium (see bibliography).

81. One practical exercise Fleming undertook in Canada was surprising a victim in a hotel room and shooting him dead. This was of course just an exercise but something Fleming was not content doing. He proved to be far from being a potential killer – so perhaps no '00' status for him there!

82. There are many official/semi-official titles for 30 AU, I opt for 30 Commando Unit and from December 1943, 30 Assault Unit in this text.

83. For Fleming's original memo regarding the formation of 30 AU see Annexe F (ADM 223/500 refers).

84. See Dalzel-Job's autobiography *Arctic Snow to Dust of Normandy, the Extraordinary Wartime Exploits of a Naval Special Agent* (Pen & Sword, 2005).

85. Otto Skorzeny was born in Vienna in 1908 and died in Madrid in 1975. He joined the Nazi Party in 1933 and became colonel of the Waffen SS during the Second World War. He achieved fame for his impressive rescue of Benito Mussolini at Campo Imperatore in the Abruzzi Mountains in 1943. He was a pioneer of False Flag Recruitment and special operations, including the training of the Werewolves. He organised the Nazi 'Ratlines' (escape routes for Nazis after the war), which became the basis of the ODESSA network, which was later brought to public attention by the work of Simon Wiesenthal and also Frederick Forsyth's novel *The Odessa File* (Hutchinson, 1972).

86. During the writing of this book I was fortunate to talk to two veterans of 30 AU, James 'Bill' Powell and Bill Thomas. They told me that to analyse 30 AU at the turn of the twenty-first Century was an incredibly difficult thing to do for several reasons: One, The D Notice stuck on each member of the unit, Two, the members of the unit being split into sections to do different jobs and, not being aware of what other sections did and, Three, because commanding officers would only tell the men a limited amount about their operations. Most veterans would be

blissfully unaware of what they were doing whilst doing it.

87.   A lot of people credit Fleming with creating this list but that is not true. He certainly contributed but Drake and Godfrey had a larger hand in its construction (they were, after all, the real Naval officers).

88.   While talking to veterans of 30 AU during the researching of this book, they were convinced that Fleming was almost instrumental in organising their 'special forces' vehicles and other equipment.

89.   For a detailed analysis of Fleming's thoughts and feeling aboard ship, see Andrew Lycett's biography *Ian Fleming* (Weidenfeld & Nicolson, 1995) which throughly documents this event.

90.   Soldiers would get more money for volunteering for Hazardous duties. (Powell/Thomas interview).

91.   Veterans Powell and Thomas remember Charles Wheeler being a fierce interrogator of enemy captors.

92.   Fleming took the unit to Scotland Yard where they learnt the art of safe blowing. From there they were sent to a big house in Buckinghamshire where they learnt much about weapons, ciphers, and intelligence gathering (along the lines of Fleming's experiences in Canada).

93.   It was mentioned to me by veterans Powell and Thomas that because of the 'hazardous' nature of their work, members of the unit were paid extra money. If they were trained for extra skills, such a parachuting, they would get even more money. Sometimes a regular soldier earned as much as a sergeant.

94.   This was something told to me by veterans Powell and Thomas, who held Fleming in such high regard, even though they never met him. They knew his reputation and what he was doing to fight their corner throughout the war and this seemed to be echoed by other men within the unit (even though 30 AU went off to do their own thing from time to time and let Fleming down – see Chapter Thirteen).

95. A little appreciated aside in *Diamonds Are Forever* has Bond tease Miss Moneypenny about a possible new boyfriend, Sefton Delmer. As Miss Moneypenny is thought to be based upon Fleming's own secretary at NID, this is quite possibly a little piece of real-life teasing. Bond quickly goes from this scene to Scotland Yard (where part of 30 AU's training would take place), so the day-to-day life in NID is sometimes portrayed in a small way in the Bond novels; but rarely more than a tantalising glimpse.

96. Another reason for documenting Dalzel-Job and moving away from the official documentation is because of the danger of including inaccuracies from the original documentation (as mentioned by senior staff on file). The problem with forming narrative largely based on Dalzel-Job's writings is secrecy. Because his work was classified secret there was only so much he could say. His autobiography loses large chunks of information; but what it does have is the human story and the bare structure of intelligence work carried out by 30 AU from his inception.

97. Such a recurring theme in the Bond novels, one does suppose Dalzel-Job was the major Bond influence.

98. Shortly after joining 30 AU Dalzel-Job met Fleming's mother on a train. He thought her 'an attractive and charming women', who told her that Fleming hoped to be an author after the war 'but she did not think he could ever make a living in that way'.

99. Veterans Powell and Thomas explain that Fleming did much in obtaining the right equipment for 30 AU. They hold him completely responsible for the depth of support that came out of Whitehall, which I can substantiate by the amount of papers on record appertaining to 'kit' for the operations of 30 AU in the field (National Archive).

100. The Fairbairn-Sykes Commando Knife (sometime spelt Fairburn-Sykes albeit incorrectly) came in three patterns. The first in limited quantities in 1941, the second, specially blackened for UK commandos and a cheaper looking third

version, also blackened. The second pattern usually has 'England' on it and the third pattern either 'England' or 'William Rogers Sheffield England'. It is speculated that most 30 AU commandos had the second pattern, characteristically with ball base, which strangely is sported as a centrepiece to the dustwrapper – and front board – of the James Bond novel *The Spy Who Loved Me*.

101. The Citadel can still be observed today. Its imposing form sits behind the Admiralty overlooking St James's Park. Donald McLachlan wrote of it: 'The Citadel quarters were admirably clean . . . cut off by twenty feet of steel and concrete from the fresh air of St James's Park and the Mall. Indeed, it was probably the best bomb proof headquarters in London . . . complete exclusion from the outside world: no windows, no daylight, no sound of traffic or birds or wind, only the noise of work being done. It was the engine room of NID.' *Room 39 – Naval Intelligence in Action 1939–45* (Weidenfeld & Nicolson, 1968).

102. The knowledge concerning D Day was rated 'Bigot', which was a classification above 'Top Secret'. One day, Dalzel-Job recalled, he was asked if he had been 'bigoted'. He said that he had and instantly fell into conversation about D Day plans – before he should have been privy to that knowledge!

103. Only the naval and Royal Marine sections of 30 AU took part in D Day (June 1944), as the Army sections were requested to take part in work being conducted by 15th Army Group in Italy.

104. Veteran Powell told me that Patton always wanted his men to wear tin helmets, 30 AU would only when absolutely necessary; but not when Patton wanted it!

105. Dalzel-Job's autobiography.

106. A shallow trench for a soldier to lay in and protect them from flying shrapnel and observation.

107. The deception papers for these operations were published by Dennis Wheatley in *Stranger Than Fiction* (Hutchinson,

1959) and brought together (in an edited version) with other documentation in *Dennis Wheatley – Churchill's Storyteller* (Spellmount, 2006) by Craig Cabell.

108. See documents listed at Annex A.

109. A good insight into the Crossbow Committee meeting can be taken from Alanbrooke's diaries (Weidenfeld & Nicolson).

110. This is an extremely important point and something that is lacking in archive material. Veterans Powell and Thomas told me that there was 'a lot' of work concerning V1s and V2s. Ralph Izzard was a guru on the subject. Also that there were scientists attached to 30 AU who were specifically interested in V2 rocket intelligence – this would fall under the remit of Operation BIG BEN, not Operation CROSSBOW – and this became an important activity for 30 AU during the latter days of the war. Powell also told me that a lot of intelligence came from Fleming as to the location of V1 and V2 rocket sites. It is Powell's belief that much of this intelligence came from the French Resistance and Fleming would filter that intelligence through to the unit that needed that intelligence. I carefully word that because in his autobiography, Dalzel-Job mentions Staff-Sergeant Bramah, the crashed glider pilot who worked with French Resistance and helped him from time to time. Dalzel-Job also mentioned that the French Resistance was very underused, which suggests that Dalzel-Job may have acquired information through Bramah, fed it back to Fleming, who made a different sector of 30 AU act upon it.

111. Baxter became known as the voice of the Farnborough Air Show and TV presenter for *Tomorrow's World*.

112. This meeting was told to the author by Irene Younghusband whilst attending the reception for Raymond Baxter's Memorial 19 April 2007 at the RAF Club, London.

113. During interview to support *Operation Big Ben – the anti-V2 Spitfire Missions, 1944-45* (Spellmount 2006) by Craig Cabell and Graham A Thomas.

114. When Operation BIG BEN was in full swing the spitfires would dive-bomb railway tracks, bridges, major roads, anywhere supplies for the rockets would come from and troops such as 30 AU would provide intelligence re locations while taking intelligence from the various bases.

115. It can be argued that a steady stream of bombing occurred over London despite the efforts of the Spitfire squadrons. I personally believe this to be a very narrow-minded opinion of a fantastically difficult mission. It is proved through squadron histories, log books, interviews (that I have undertaken) and other general conversations, that the amount of rockets that fell on London would have greatly increased if it wasn't for the Spitfires blowing up supply line, lorries, rocket sites and individuals through low level/dive-bombing activities.

116. When the book *Operation Big Ben* was released by Spellmount to the press in late 2005, Raymond Baxter agreed to undertake interviews to support the book because questions were asked about the authenticity of the operation. As Baxter flew in the mission and was a respected aviation expert (since the war) he felt it important to endorse the operation via interview, special introduction to the book and a book signing at a mini-launch in Duxford (where seven Spitfires flew on the day) also attended by Lady Bader as the second guest of honour. These activities prove how difficult it is to authenticate a once covert operation sixty years after it happened and, it is felt, that 30 AU fall into a similar trap as their work was covert for so long.

117. Released in 3 volumes under the main title *The Time Has Come...* (Hutchinson, 1977, 78 and 79). See also *The Deception Planners* (Hutchinson 1980) for other work appertaining to JPS, LCS.

118. Photographs of these recces are still banned from publication, some of which still reside in private hands.

119. 30 AU did feel that they were the bees knees. In July 1944

the unit served in Rennes and Brest and then followed Free French Forces into Paris during the liberation of the city in August. They would have acquired many first hand perceptions from the people they met along the road and formed an opinion effectively based upon Chinese whispers and half-truths.

120. Coincidently Fleming wanted his cousin Christopher Lee to play Dr No in the movie, but he didn't get his way. Lee would eventually play another Fleming character after the author had died: Scaramanga in *The Man With the Golden Gun*.

121. On his way to Gibraltar (during the planning of Operation Goldeneye), Fleming found time to relax by playing bridge with Joan Bright, Jean Crawford and General Ismay (who were travelling by ship for different reasons). Bridge was a social pastime for Fleming where he could meet up with friends (see Joan Bright's *The Inner Circle, A View of War at the Top*, Hutchinson, 1971).

122. Edited version of enclosure from ADM 223/2, referenced ZIP/ZG/12.

123. In August 1944 an A5 booklet was written entitled *Intelligence Assault Force Operations*, it showcased how to organise and implement a unit such as 30 AU. The practices detailed, are exactly as laid down by Fleming (at the beginning of Annexe) in his memo. A copy of the booklet resides in ADM 223/214.

124. This memo from Godfrey opens file ADM 223/214, but a lot of the history of 30 AU as laid down in the file is discredited by DDNI Colonel H Quill RM. With 30 AU, like the SOE, there was much bad blood amongst the military. However, there are some factual inaccuracies in the main documented history as laid down in the file. I have only taken uncontentious facts for my chapters that concern 30 AU.

Index